The Propaganda of Peace

In memory of Louis McLaughlin and Mervyn Baker

The Propaganda of Peace
The Role of Media and Culture in the Northern Ireland Peace Process

Greg McLaughlin and Stephen Baker

intellect Bristol, UK / Chicago, USA

First published in the UK in 2010 by
Intellect, The Mill, Parnall Road, Fishponds, Bristol, BS16 3JG, UK

First published in the USA in 2010 by
Intellect, The University of Chicago Press, 1427 E. 60th Street,
Chicago, IL 60637, USA

A catalogue record for this book is available from the
British Library.

Cover designer: Holly Rose
Copy-editor: Andrew Duncan
Typesetting: Mac Style, Beverley, E. Yorkshire

ISBN 978-1-84150-272-4

Printed and bound by Gutenberg Press, Malta.

Contents

Contents

Acknowledgements

We would like to thank all those whose support and encouragement have been crucial to the research, writing and completion of this book. Of special importance were Intellect Books for their faith in the project, especially Sam King, James Campbell, Jennifer Schivas and Andrew Duncan; the material and intellectual support of the Centre for Media Research at the University of Ulster, particularly the leadership and expertise of Professors Maire Messenger Davies and Martin McLoone; the comments and suggestions throughout the project from our colleagues, Cahal McLaughlin, Bill Rolston and the legendary Bobbie Porter; the generous book-development grant from the University's Research Office; the photos and copyright permissions from Pacemaker Press International in Belfast; and the staff at the Linen Hall and Central Libraries, Belfast. We offer special thanks to our friend and Head of School, Sarah Edge, for carving out valuable time for us in the run-up to the submission deadline. Thanks, also, to our families and friends who wondered many times about our sanity and absences but showed us nothing but love, faith and understanding, especially Alice, Kathryn, Nye and Ewan. As for the two Maureens; your boys did good didn't they?

Chapter 1

Defining the Propaganda of Peace

Bono, Trimble and Hume. Pacemaker Press International Limited

This book is about the propaganda of peace in Northern Ireland that was mobilised during the period that led to the ratification of the Good Friday Agreement 1998, and that has helped to sustain the peace process ever since. The propaganda of peace is the work of a variety of social forces through a range of media and cultural forms, and its purpose is to bring society, culture or nation behind a core idea or principle, in this case, the promise of peace and its economic dividends after decades of conflict. It is therefore a conception of propaganda that is broader than that usually associated with war, when it tends to be systematically organised by the state, the national military or paramilitary organisations. While institutions of the state play a key role in the propaganda of peace, they act in concert with other hegemonic social forces, such as local businesses and political elites, trade unions, the voluntary and community sector, academia and the media. Persuading for peace is no less propaganda because of its association with civil society and its apparently benign intentions, for it displays a coherent set of ideas and values that seek to mobilise people to act and behave in the interests of power.

A good illustration of this is the image opposite, widely circulated by the media just three days before the referendum that would ratify the Good Friday Agreement in 1998. The moment: global superstar Bono of U2 holds aloft the arms of David Trimble and John Hume, leaders of unionism and nationalism respectively, like they are two triumphant prize-fighters; at long last, after thirty years of conflict, they are working together as 'persuaders for peace'. The occasion: a peace concert in Belfast, hastily staged by a local entertainments promoter in support of the Yes Campaign. The venue: the new Waterfront Hall, status symbol of the economic and cultural regeneration of Belfast. The audience: a selection of high-schoolchildren from across the sectarian divide in the city who, although too young to vote in the referendum, stand as a poignant, optimistic symbol of the future.

The appearance of Trimble and Hume together on stage with Bono was a rapturous moment but one that has since served as shorthand for the essential meaning of the peace process. Writing on the tenth anniversary of the concert, Stuart Bailie, a local broadcaster and music journalist, reflected on its significance:

I occasionally ask myself that if Bono hadn't encouraged Trimble and Hume to shake hands ten years ago, would we currently have peace in Northern Ireland? This might seem like a facetious idea, but really, if the 'Yes' referendum had died back then, the centre ground might also have perished. We could still be living in a mean, fractious place. We might not have witnessed the housing boom, the construction fever and the arrival of Wagamama. (Bailie 2008)[1]

Bailie is certain that the moment saved the Agreement and Northern Ireland from an 'uncertain nightmare' but his association of political accord with rising property prices and the arrival of international retail chains is just as interesting as his bold claims about the impact of the concert. In this he is not alone. A constant refrain in public debate about the peace process was the 'peace dividend': the promise of economic prosperity and the consumer nirvana that would ensue from a political settlement. The propaganda of peace, then, was only partly about encouraging accord between unionism and nationalism. It had another purpose: to prepare Northern Ireland for integration into global capitalism, something barely acknowledged in public debate where the Good Friday Agreement was rarely considered as anything other than a self-evident good.

Political context: The Good Friday Agreement

The consociational arrangements the Agreement provided for, and within which Ulster unionists and Irish nationalists share power, are seen as an historic compromise; a peace settlement; a blueprint for the resolution of conflicts elsewhere; and the precursor to prosperity. Those who oppose the Agreement usually do so because they see it as a betrayal of either Ulster unionist or Irish republican principle. However, when we consider the context within which the Agreement was forged we get a clearer picture of what it represents.

A starting point for this might be comments made by the then British Prime Minister, Tony Blair, in July 1999, during negotiations aimed at implementing the Agreement. The negotiations had stalled on the issue of republican decommissioning and the inclusion of Sinn Féin in a power-sharing executive. Frustrated by the lack of progress, Blair told reporters that: 'The entire civilised world will not understand if we can't put this together and make it work. They simply won't understand and rightly'.[2] Of course, the 'civilised world' he referred to emerged at the end of the Cold War, a new world order that accepted the triumph of capitalism and liberal democracy. Ben-Porat highlights the proliferation of peace studies during this period and 'the attempts of regional and core powers to devise and influence peace in local, off-centre yet important conflicts' such as those the Middle East and Northern Ireland. Crucial to this was the link between peace and economic growth. The promise of a 'peace dividend' in the form of global integration motivated business communities and their allies actively to support efforts towards political settlement.

There were other political pressures brought to bear on the conflict in Northern Ireland specifically. The antagonism that once existed between the Irish and British establishments subsided as the two states became partners in Europe. The growing European Union combined with globalisation put into question the very idea of national sovereignty, which impacted upon Northern Ireland's conflicting national allegiances. In response, moderates like those in the Social Democratic and Labour Party (SDLP) began to think about a possible resolution to the conflict in decidedly post-nationalist terms, proposing that Northern Ireland's identity crisis could be resolved within a 'Europe of the regions'.

Similar ideas accompanied devolution in Scotland and Wales, where the economic success of the Republic of Ireland within Europe acted as an inspiration. Also, the rise of the Celtic Tiger, 'the break up of Britain', as well as the assumed erosion of national sovereignty, undermined the constitutional and economic logic of Ulster unionism, which was slower than nationalism to respond to, or embrace, the new times. It is precisely this conjuncture of political and historical specifics that made the Good Friday Agreement possible. The political raison d'être of Irish nationalism and Ulster unionism in Northern Ireland was no longer sustainable or containable.

Research context

It is in this context that we examine the role of media and cultural representation in Northern Ireland during the period of the peace process, a time when its image and reputation changed remarkably. Pictures and stories of interminable conflict were replaced by representations apparently more befitting a place undergoing the transition from violent conflict to peace; from a democratic deficit to a working democratic settlement; and from over-dependence on government subvention to enterprise economy. However, there is a paradox here in that these extraordinary transformations in Northern Irish society have been attended by the truncation of political debate and the impoverishment of the cultural imagination. In the course of a peace process that has been called 'the only show in town', dissenting voices have been marginalised or maligned, political activism viewed as disruptive of the social order and pacified domesticity presented as the preferred model of citizenship. Our purpose, therefore, is not merely to describe or catalogue media representations of peace but to unpack and expose the tensions and contradictions contained within them.

Much of the academic literature on the media's role in representing the conflict in Northern Ireland serves to illuminate but also sometimes constrict our understanding of the media's deeper, ideological role. With perhaps the exceptions of *Televising 'Terrorism'* (Schlesinger et al 1983), Miller's edited collection *Rethinking Northern Ireland* (1998) and Rolston's series on political murals, *Drawing Support* (1992, 1995 and 2003), this work is focused rather narrowly on the news media, the assumption being that they are the most significant in terms of propaganda and censorship, shaping public understanding and facilitating political debate.[3] Other scholars have looked at film and television representations of Ireland, including Northern Ireland;[4] or specifically Northern Ireland.[5]

While valuable in its own right, this body of research rather underestimates or neglects the role and significance of other media and cultural forms, not just in terms of their particular representations but also in how they work in symphony to communicate a propaganda message. The critical departure for this book is that it considers not just news, current affairs and government propaganda but also other representations found in film, television drama and situation comedy, public exhibitions, public access broadcasting and alternative media.

The virtue of looking across a broad cross-section of media and cultural forms is that it allows us to understand how propaganda is found in the relatively 'closed' forms of news and current affairs, where state intervention is most obvious, but is also complemented by more 'open' forms such as drama and comedy. Indeed its location in these 'open' forms is precisely what might make it all the more persuasive because of its assumed distance from 'official' thinking (Schlesinger et al 1983). Nevertheless what this study highlights is the unity and coherence of the propaganda of peace whatever its source. We are not suggesting that there is a conspiracy or an entirely self-conscious effort to sue for a particular version of peace. Rather we are suggesting that cultural forms and conventions can articulate an emerging 'structure of feeling' at a particular historical moment (Williams 1961, 1977 and 1979). This is a concept we will return to in our concluding chapter.

Outline

Our analysis begins in chapter 2 by setting the concept of 'the propaganda of peace' in the context of news reporting of the negotiations towards a political settlement: the so-called 'first draft of history'. It examines how the local press responded to key moments of crisis and breakthrough in the process since the Good Friday Agreement, and identifies in their reporting the development of a particular narrative, one that entirely accepted the government's view that there was 'no plan B' should the process fail. The Northern Ireland daily newspapers all recommended a Yes vote in the referendum of 1998 to copper-fasten the Agreement, fearing as the only alternative a return to conflict. In this respect, the 'first draft of history' was linear, didactic and predetermined, thus serving to constrict public debate and marginalise alternative points of view.

While chapter 2 looks at the 'first draft of history' as laid down in news and journalism, chapter 3 examines how the past serves the ideological needs of the present. This is not just a question of history and its narrative. The form of its public exhibition is also critical, as illustrated by the commemoration of the 1798 United Irish rebellion at the Ulster Museum. The *Up in Arms* exhibition opened at the start of April 1998, days before the signing of the Agreement and offered a version of the past conducive to the peace process. Crucially it was an 'official', institutionalised history, encouraging an 'objective' gaze at the past. However, a subsequent exhibition at the museum has preferred a variety of subjective accounts, drawing upon the testimonies and reflections of selected individuals. This personal perspective may seem more democratic on the surface but it does raise the question: what will become of public history if it is presented as competing but equally legitimate personal points of view? The role and representation of the personal is central to the concerns of the two subsequent chapters.

Chapter 4 addresses one of the key problems for all those involved in resolving the conflict: how to transform negative public perceptions of the paramilitaries. The British government took a lead in this by changing the tone of its official propaganda, projecting the paramilitaries in a relatively more positive light than during the 1970s and 1980s. It prepared the public for the inclusion in the political process of one-time combatants and simultaneously sent a clear message to the paramilitaries that they could be part of a political settlement. Set in historical context, the transformation of the paramilitaries' image and reputation is remarkable. For instance, when in 1985 Martin McGuinness appeared in the BBC's *Real Lives* documentary, 'At the Edge of the Union' (BBC 1985), his portrayal as a 'family man' provoked public controversy. However by the early 1990s and with the emergence of the peace process, current affairs broadcasting, films (*The Boxer* – Sheridan 1997) and TV dramas (*Love Lies Bleeding* – Winterbottom 1993) transformed the image of paramilitaries from psychotic pariahs to politicians or 'ordinary people' in more familiar, domestic contexts. The chapter will consider the problems and contradictions that these changing images present for those searching for a clear understanding of the transition from war to peace.

The category of 'ordinary people' is commonly seen as incidental to the conflict in Northern Ireland. Yet, not only has it been critical in transforming the image of the paramilitary, it has also helped define the quality and constitution of the peace. Chapter 5 considers fictional and non-fictional media representations of apparently 'ordinary people' caught up in the conflict. Films such as *Some Mother's Son* (George 1996), *Titanic Town* (Michell 1998) and *Divorcing Jack* (Caffrey 1998), and TV dramas such as *Holy Cross* (Brozel 2003) all feature lead protagonists who must extricate themselves from political or sectarian violence and return to a private, domestic space apparently free of politics. The implications of this narrative closure are instructive: peace is the absence of politics rather than the re-imagination of political and democratic arrangements. However, this liberal notion of how 'ordinary people' conduct themselves contrasts with the more overt political agendas of public access broadcasting and of community, grassroots and alternative media, which demonstrate that there is nothing extraordinary about politics.

We end in chapter 6 by addressing a set of critical issues arising out of our analysis. For example, we do not take for granted that the propaganda of peace is purely pragmatic in its orientation; in other words, that it is solely dedicated to promoting political accord between Northern Ireland's sectarian antagonists. Rather we consider the possibility of a deeper ideological purpose, which may be to interpellate Northern Ireland within the political and cultural milieu of contemporary capitalism; after all, its denial of politics may be conducive to this end. Whatever the optimistic promise of a 'peace dividend' we should consider the very real possibility that Northern Ireland's exposure to the free-market, after so many years of financial subvention, might deepen the divisions between rich and poor as it has elsewhere in the world.

Media discussion about this sort of social division is muted. This may be because it is of little immediate concern to the middle-class intelligentsia, well represented in the media and for whom the Good Friday Agreement is seen as a delightful transformation of its own material existence and cultural experience. In the end, we ask whether the propaganda of peace actually promotes the abandonment of a politically engaged public sphere at the very moment when public debate about neo-liberalism, financial meltdown and social and economic inequality make it most necessary.

Notes

1. Bailie, Stuart (2008), 'Shake, rattle and roll', http://www.bbc.co.uk/blogs/stuartbailie/2008/03/yes.shtml. Accessed 18 August 2009.
2. Quoted in *The Irish Times*, 2 July 1999
3. See for example: Butler 1995; Curtis 1988 and 1996; Miller 1993, 1994 and 2002; McLaughlin 2000 and 2009; McLaughlin and Miller 1996; McLoone 1996; Parkinson 1998; Rolston 1991; Rolston and Miller 1996; Spencer 2000 and 2001; and Wolfsfeld 2004.
4. See for example: Barton 2004; Hill et al 1994; Pettitt 2000; Rockett et al 1987; and McLoone 2000 and 2008.
5. See for example: Baker 2004; Hill 2006; and McIlroy 1998.

Chapter 2

Framing the Good Friday Agreement

The aim of this chapter is to look at local, daily newspaper coverage of three key and critical moments in the peace process: the Good Friday Agreement of 1998; the referendum seeking popular endorsement of the Agreement, held in May 1998; and the St Andrews Agreement of 2006, which was necessary to restore the devolved institutions suspended in 2002 after a series of political crises.

Our principal focus of analysis here is on the three Belfast daily newspapers – the *Belfast Telegraph*, the *News Letter* and the *Irish News*. The *Belfast Telegraph* is moderately unionist in editorial policy but reaches a cross-community readership by virtue of its advertising and consumer content. At the time of the Agreement it was a multi-edition evening paper with sales of more than 100,000 copies per day. Since then, it has undergone a change of ownership (bought by Dublin-based Independent News and Media) and publishes a morning edition in tabloid format. However, it has also experienced a drastic fall in sales to just over 68,000 per day. The *News Letter*, traditionally the voice of official Ulster Unionism, has also experienced a dramatic collapse in political influence and circulation in the past 60 years, falling from more than 100,000 copies, post-Second World War, to 25,000 today. The paper has changed ownership twice since 1996 and is now owned by the Scottish media group, Johnston Press Plc. The *Irish News* has a daily circulation of 46,800 copies but has not suffered the drastic decline in sales experienced by its unionist counterparts. It is privately owned by the Fitzpatrick family and promotes an editorial line broadly supportive of the moderate, nationalist Social and Democratic Labour Party (SDLP).[1]

We also compared coverage of the Belfast daily newspapers with the alternative publications of radical or dissident political groups, especially those associated with republican and loyalist paramilitaries. We wanted to see if the framework of interpretation constructed by the mainstream local press truly reflected the attitude and mood among their unionist and nationalist readerships or if their coverage was informed more by a restricted consensus in favour of the Good Friday Agreement and the political settlement it implied. These alternative publications offered us a useful perspective from which to make this assessment; our source for them was the Political Collection of the Linen Hall Library in Belfast.

The Good Friday Agreement

We looked at daily newspaper coverage of the Good Friday Agreement, including the last stage of negotiations and the aftermath, a sample period of four days from Thursday 9 April to Monday 13 April 1998 (excluding Sunday 12 April). We wanted to identify the narrative themes arising from the coverage of each newspaper, specifically and chiefly from front-page headlines, news items, photo features and editorial content.

In the coverage of the Agreement, we identified three shifting themes, starting with the 'political thriller' of the negotiations between the political parties inside government buildings at Stormont, then changing to 'the epic' narrative of the Agreement they reached on Good Friday, 10 April, followed by the 'hard sell' of the Agreement to constituency parties and the broader population of Northern Ireland. Our analysis that follows is qualitative, not quantitative, and as such is in line with the broad, methodological rationale used throughout this volume.

Setting the scene

As negotiations for the Agreement reached a critical climax, media attention intensified, with a large local and international media presence camped outside government buildings at Stormont, where the talks took place. Much of this coverage consisted of routine reporting on the ground that depended upon sources inside – party negotiators or press officers and government officials. This factor alone, we would argue, had some significant bearing on the hyperbolic and fluid language used to describe the negotiations, with party sources having some stake in communicating to the public their determination not to compromise on core principles. Adding some dramatic colour to proceedings was the fact that one of the parties, the Democratic Unionist Party (DUP), led by the Reverend Ian Paisley, chose not to take part in the negotiations because of their opposition to the very idea of a power-sharing agreement with Sinn Féin, a party they regarded as a public front for the IRA. The spectacle, therefore, of tense, difficult negotiations between Unionist and Nationalist parties inside and the spectre of uncompromising, hardline Unionism looming outside, provided some ready-made copy for journalists who spent much of their time starved of real information about talks that were meant to be secret.[2]

From political thriller to historic epic

The headlines on the progress of the negotiations give an immediate impression of the tone of the coverage throughout this period. Front page news reports on Thursday 9 April conveyed the sense of pressure building inside government buildings as party negotiators remained 'locked in strenuous eleventh hour efforts [with] the clock ticking away towards the [government-imposed] deadline' for agreement (News Letter, 9 April 1998). Colourful imagery and mixed metaphors abounded. The 'high wire' political talks were 'on a cliff edge' (Irish News, 9 April 1998) as negotiators 'battled against the clock' to agree on the 'political landmines' of policing, weapons decommissioning and prisoner releases according to 'a loyalist source' (Belfast Telegraph, 9 April 1998).

Thursday 9 April was set to be 'Ulster's longest day' (*News Letter*, 9 April 1998) with negotiations 'So near and yet so far' from agreement (*Irish News*, 9 April 1998). An early edition of the *Belfast Telegraph* led on page one with 'North-South bodies deal' (9 April 1998), reporting a breakthrough on Strand Two of the draft document concerning the creation of North-South public bodies, only to report in a later edition that 'North-South deal hits snag' (9 April 1998).

As negotiations edged closer to agreement throughout Thursday and well into Good Friday, the tone of newspaper coverage perceptibly shifted from political thriller to the epic themes of hope and history. The headlines on Good Friday announced that it was to be 'Destiny Day' and 'An historic time for Northern Ireland' (*Belfast Telegraph*, 10 April 1998); 'A moment of history' in which the people stood 'at a crossroads in Irish history' (*Irish News*, 'A moment of history', 10 April 1998); that Ulster 'seemed to be on the verge of a challenging, if uncertain, new future' (*News Letter*, 10 April 1998) and that it was 'on the brink of an historic agreement' (*Belfast Telegraph*, 10 April 1998). With reference to past conflicts resolved, the *Belfast Telegraph* leader asked: 'Can we dismantle the Berlin Walls within all our minds? Can we, British and Irish alike, break down the barriers of political and religious apartheid that have beset this island for too long? [...] It is now up to the people to provide a final answer otherwise this province will consign itself to the wilderness of European history' (10 April 1998).

Yet some of the imagery suggested a degree of uncertainty among the papers about whether a deal was really possible. The *Irish News* reported that negotiations were 'on a knife-edge [...] with an historic settlement in sight' (*Irish News*, 10 April 1998). The *News Letter* declared that 'Historic bartering goes right to the wire' (10 April 1998), while the *Belfast Telegraph* warned readers that 'Northern Ireland has seen many false dawns, which have ended in tragedy' (10 April 1998).

In tandem with the epic language of history-making, the newspapers were mindful of the religious and spiritual context of what was taking place at Stormont. The *Belfast Telegraph* ('An Easter of hope') thought it was 'truly Good Friday' and that 'There could be no more appropriate occasion for [...] an historic agreement than on the eve of Easter, with its message of hope and revival' (10 April 1998). The paper carried a front-page photo feature that juxtaposed images of two women at prayer in Belfast – one a Catholic, the other a Protestant – with the caption: 'Joined in faith, united in prayer for peace' (10 April 1998). The *Irish News* reflected that while it was important 'that we do not confuse the spiritual message of Easter with the political one', this Easter 'could be a turning point in our lives and the lives of our fellow citizens' (10 April 1998).

Selling the Agreement

After the initial euphoria and international acclaim that greeted the Agreement, events and developments on the ground suggested that coming to an agreement was one thing, selling it to broader political and popular constituencies in Northern Ireland was quite another. Hard and fast agreement was not actually reached until 5pm on Good Friday after some members of the Ulster Unionist negotiating team walked out on their leader, David Trimble. Indeed, it was Trimble who faced the most difficult challenge of selling the Agreement to the party rank and file, which would have to ratify it formally before it could be presented to the people in a referendum. Sinn Féin president, Gerry Adams, would also have to gain approval from his party at a special party conference (Ard Fheis). The prospect inspired dramatic copy for the newspapers.

On Easter Saturday, 11 April, the *Belfast Telegraph* headlined with 'Trouble in the Trimble ranks. Leader heading off party revolt', while the *News Letter* led with 'Trimble facing revolt'. On Monday 13 April, the *Irish News* devoted the large part of its front page to two stories about the challenge facing both leaders. The reports stand in marked contrast to each other in tone and language, giving a very different impression of the nature of the challenge and the political parties involved. Under the headline, 'Crunch time for Trimble', the story at the top of the page reported that the Ulster Unionist leader faced 'a revolt [in] the most crucial week of his political life' and 'stormy questions' from rebel MPs at a forthcoming meeting of the parliamentary party (13 April 1998). One of the most vocal and virulent of his opponents, MP Willie Thompson, told the *Irish News* that there would be an 'awful struggle' in both the party and the unionist electorate. In fact, he said, 'This is bad enough to destroy Ulster'. The United Ulster Council, a fledgling opposition lobby group, released a statement to the paper in which it urged unionists to 'rise to the challenge and defeat the evil and treacherous forces that are hell bent on our destruction'.

For Gerry Adams and Sinn Féin, the story was one of internal consensus and consultation rather than dissent and rebellion. Under the headline, 'Sinn Féin plays for time on deal', the *Irish News* article reported on Adams' speech to a republican Easter rally in Carrickmore, County Tyrone, in which the key terms were 'consultation', 'consideration', and 'future strategy and policy' (13 April 1998). This was supported by a statement from the IRA, promising to 'carefully study' the Agreement document. If there was any dissent in republican ranks, it was not hinted at in this report, suggesting a much more disciplined and managed response to developments than from unionism.

The task selling the deal to the people was foremost in the minds of copy editors and editorial writers who appeared to be inspired by background briefings from the Northern Ireland Office (NIO), such was the similarity in tone and language. On Saturday, 11 April, the *Belfast Telegraph* reminded readers that 'the real work is yet to come'; the *News Letter*, that 'The hard work is only beginning'; the *Irish News*, that 'Today is only the beginning, it is not the end', that 'The real work begins now' and that 'in truth, the hard work is just beginning'. By Monday, 13 April, the papers were making direct appeals to readers to make their own minds up ahead of a likely referendum on the Agreement. In its editorial – 'Selling the Agreement' – the *Belfast Telegraph* warned that 'People must form their own opinion and should not allow themselves to be unduly influenced by the soundbite comments of various politicians', rather that they make 'informed rather than emotional judgements'. The *News*

Letter took its cue from British Prime Minister, Tony Blair, with the emphatic front page headline, underlined and white against black, 'Seize this chance', reporting Blair's advice that 'the voices of opposition should be ignored' (13 April 1998).

If we look at coverage of the referendum of 22 May, it appears that the local dailies followed Blair's advice when it came to directing people which way to vote; and that they ignored their own advice about the pitfalls of soundbite politics. Indeed, it became very clear that the media were to play a key role as what the *Irish News* called 'persuaders for peace' (22 May 1998). In keeping with the official line, there was to be no alternative to the Agreement, no Plan B if it failed – two propositions that became very questionable over the next few years of the peace process.

The referendum

What is remarkable about coverage of the referendum is the concerted campaign by all three Belfast dailies to recommend a Yes vote in support of the Agreement, despite the evident scepticism about the Agreement within broader unionist and loyalist communities.

Recommending the Yes vote

On the eve of the referendum poll, the *Belfast Telegraph* headline, 'The final push' (21 May 1998), was supported by a strapline quote from Tony Blair – 'This deal is right, just and proper' – and a photo of him overseeing a handshake between David Trimble and John Hume, captioned: 'Yes campaign: Blair, Trimble and Hume stand together' (even though the objections of the No campaign were not to powersharing with moderate nationalism but with republicanism). The paper also featured on the front page of this edition the first paragraph of its editorial headed, 'Why we say Yes', in which it referred to 'a day of destiny and decision for everyone' (21 May 1998). The *News Letter* and *Irish News* both led with Tony Blair's last-minute handwritten pledge to the people of Northern Ireland promising that no one linked to violence would be allowed to sit on the executive or in the assembly: 'Chance of a lifetime' (*News Letter*, 21 May 1998), and 'Blair makes final plea for Agreement support' (*Irish News*, 21 May 1998).

On referendum day, the papers moved into top gear. Most spectacular of all was the *News Letter*, which devoted its entire front page to an emphatic headline, underlined and white-on-black: 'Say Yes and say it loud!' The page was footed with a mock-up ballot paper with an X marking the preference for the Yes vote. The *Irish News* headline, 'Let the people decide' framed another photo of Blair, Trimble and Hume, captioned: 'Yes Agreement: David Trimble, Tony Blair and John Hume are confident that a majority of the North's voters will endorse the Mitchell agreement today' (22 May 1998). The *Belfast Telegraph* was published at that time as an evening paper and so picked up on early indications of the projected turn-out. Its headline, 'Record poll. Ulster voters face historic moment of truth. Queues in streets as people rush to have their say', framed a photograph of a man carrying a child past a NIO billboard advertisement featuring the front cover of the Agreement document that had been distributed to the public in advance of the poll and stamped with the handwritten referendum slogan, 'It's _Your_ Choice'. The photo feature was captioned: 'Future hopes: An Ulster father and child walk past an Agreement poster today'.

The editorials supporting these front-page recommendations were also remarkable for the similarities in language and tone. The core message common to them all was inspired by Tony Blair's previous public pronouncements that 'the hand of history' was on the people's shoulders, that the 'civilised world' would not forgive them and leave them behind if they delivered anything other than an unambiguous Yes and that there was no alternative, no Plan B.

The *Belfast Telegraph* editorial on the eve of poll – 'Why we say Yes' – was constructed with one eye to the past and one to the future, referring to Blair's 'hand of history' and to 22 June 1922, when King George addressed the first Northern Ireland parliament and appealed for conciliation and forgiveness among all the people of Ireland, North and South, regardless of creed, national identity or politics. The referendum, said the paper, was a chance for the people to realise this aspiration at long last. It told its readers that 'The choice is yours and the decision is in your hands' but then went on to advise them that the 'prize can only be achieved by making a leap of faith and voting Yes tomorrow'. The paper concluded that there could be no alternative – 'Can we really think of another way?' – and declared that, 'The moment has come to grasp the hand of history. Let Ulster say Yes at last!' (21 May 1998). As voters went to the polls the next day, its editorial was headed, 'Vote Yes. Decision Day: Stand up and be counted'. It acknowledged that 'The world is now awaiting Northern Ireland's verdict' and that anything but a resounding Yes vote would be 'interpreted [...] by the wider world as signifying that unionists want to retreat into the past'. On that basis, it concluded, 'The future lies in our own hands and we must grasp the opportunity which is presented. For once, let the world hear a resounding Yes from Ulster' (22 May 1998).

The *News Letter* editorial on the eve of the poll – 'Time for confidence to say and vote Yes' – acknowledged the fears and anxieties in the unionist family as expressed by the No campaign but pointed out what unionism had to lose by voting No. 'For the sake of future generations we cannot say NO. They, and history, might never forgive us' (21 May 1998). Like the *Belfast Telegraph*, the paper's editorial on referendum day – 'Why we must say Yes' – pulled a rhetorical sleight of hand. Having explained at length why there was no alternative to voting Yes, it ended by telling its readers: 'Today it's up to you'. The unionist people had the chance to become no less than 'the architects and the artisans of a New Model Ulster' (22 May 1998).

The *Irish News* editorial on the eve of the poll – 'A new era is within reach' – saw the coming vote as one that could 'prove to be a turning point in our history'. Working out the Agreement in practice would not be easy, it concluded, 'but an equitable solution is within our grasp. A strong Yes vote tomorrow is the key' (21 May 1998). Its editorial on referendum day, headed 'Time to trust each other', referred directly to an adjacent op-ed article by Tony Blair ('The North's fresh start on a fair and equitable basis'). It recognised the crucial role Blair played in the peace process and supported his view that 'we can only make progress through the Good Friday Agreement if we start to trust each other. A convincing Yes vote in today's referendum will offer us all the chance to take an enormous step in that direction' (22 May 1998).

Acclaiming the result

By close of polling on 22 May, it was evident from exit polls that, with a record high turn-out of between 85 and 90% of the electorate, there was a decisive overall Yes vote in the North of 70–75%. However, a breakdown of the voting suggested that the unionist vote was evenly split, 50-50 as against a unanimous Yes vote from nationalists of 99%. (In the Republic, 95% of a very high turn-out voted in favour of the Agreement.) Despite this worrying disparity between unionist and nationalist voting, all three Belfast dailies devoted their front pages to the story the day after, accentuating the positive and playing down unionist reserve: 'The people give their verdict: It's Yes. Massive poll gives a resounding result' (*Belfast Telegraph*, 23 May 1998); 'Smile that means Yes – record turn outs as Ulster stampedes to polls' (*News Letter*, 23 May 1998); 'Ireland says Yes' (*Irish News*, 23 May 1998).

The editorials emphasised the historic and decisive implications of the result. The *News Letter* – 'A proud people standing on the edge of history' – focused almost entirely on the implications of the result for unionism, reminding readers that whatever the imperfections of the Good Friday Agreement, 'it has the ability to bring the two people together in a positive way [and] that the rest of the civilised world is changing, old conflicts are being laid to rest, new beginnings are being made' (23 May 1998). The *Belfast Telegraph* editorial – 'Historic Yes. The verdict: A bright new dawn for Northern Ireland' – said that, 'The voters of Northern Ireland have spoken and their verdict is an emphatic Yes to the Good Friday agreement'. It was a result that vindicated David Trimble's battle to 'assuage the fears of the unionist community and to deploy logic in the face of the emotional arguments put forward by the No campaign'. In an echo of the coverage of the Good Friday Agreement, the paper warned that while the referendum had been won, 'the real contest is yet to come in the form of assembly elections'. Ultimately, however, 'the voters of Northern Ireland have sent out a message to the world that they are no longer prepared to be prisoners of the past' (23 May 1998).

Unlike its rivals, the *Irish News* did not devote its editorial to the result on the morning after but its usual Saturday column by James Kelly, headed 'Goodbye to the past, hello bright future', opened with the declaration that 'History was made yesterday. The people of Ireland voted to end the war and get on with our lives, leaving the dismal past behind us' (23 May 1998). The bulk of the column dismissed the arguments and criticisms of the No campaign led by the Reverend Ian Paisley and Bob McCartney, founder and leader of the tiny UK Unionist

Party. Adjacent to the editorial was a cartoon by Ian Knox that depicts some of the heroes and villains of Irish nationalist history – Wolfe Tone, Robert Emmet, Daniel O'Connell, Michael Collins, Eamon de Valera and Edward Carson – standing around in triumphant poses with their fingers crossed, presumably for the right vote in the referendum.

In 2006, a year after IRA decommissioning, the parties gathered at St Andrews, Scotland, for talks to restore devolution. By this time, the moderate centre, represented by the Ulster Unionist Party (UUP) and the SDLP, had been overtaken in the polls by the DUP and Sinn Féin. With the emergence of the so-called extremes as the largest parties, it was expected that negotiations would be difficult. The issues to be resolved included the devolution of justice powers, which for the DUP was conditional upon Sinn Féin's explicit support for policing. However, the prospect of agreement would not sit easily with the rank and file of the DUP. For so long, Ian Paisley led them in staunch opposition to sharing power with republicans. Now, with Sinn Féin becoming more and more mainstream and moderate in its policies and attitudes, it was becoming more difficult for him to keep saying no.

The St Andrews Agreement

The negotiations that unfolded at St Andrews were mediated by the two governments in the persons of Tony Blair and Irish Prime Minister (Taoiseach) Bertie Ahern. After years of political new dawns and disasters, they finally appeared to be wielding the stick rather than the carrot. The message they put out to the parties sounded uncompromising: come to a deal to restore devolution or face an indefinite period of joint stewardship by the two governments, in which painful decisions on health, education, justice and local government would be taken out of your hands. Nonetheless, the DUP and Sinn Féin in particular were keen to maintain the dual strategy of being seen to be hardline in public but flexible and accommodating in private. This meant that the talks followed the familiar, tidal pattern as those leading to the Good Friday Agreement, where hopes of a final deal ebbed and flowed right to the deadline imposed by the two governments.

Reporting the talks: breakthroughs, deadlocks and breakthroughs

In contrast to their united and unqualified support for the Good Friday Agreement, and their strong recommendation of a Yes vote in the referendum, the three Belfast dailies were much more cautious and downbeat in their coverage of the St Andrews summit and eventual agreement. At first, they tried to track each and every 'breakthrough' or 'deadlock' as if they were conclusive without any explicit acknowledgement that this was in the nature of any form of negotiation to solve a dispute.

The *News Letter* and *Irish News* were remarkable for the extent to which they took their cues from the two governments. On the first day of coverage, the *News Letter* led on its front page with a bullish statement by Tony Blair: 'It's got to be done!' (11 October 2006), while the *Irish News* featured an interview with Northern Ireland Secretary of State, Peter Hain, in which he sent out a similar hardline message: 'I have found that when I have been out and about in Northern Ireland that everybody is urging me not to blink – and we won't – as governments' (11 October 2006). The two papers continued to privilege this official line throughout their coverage of the talks: 'Deal or no deal, this is your last time' (*News Letter*, 12 October 2006); 'Blair and Ahern expected to tell parties – Take it or leave it' (*Irish News*, 13 October 2006).

On the eve of the talks, 11 October, the newspapers set out the key issues that needed to be resolved. The *Belfast Telegraph* led with one of its stock phrases to match such occasions: 'Day of Destiny – one hotel, two governments, 70 politicians […] and the hopes and fears of 1.7 million people'. Inside, it noted that the talks at St Andrews would began on the exact anniversary of the suspension of the Assembly and Executive in 2002: 'Since then, it has been the dark night of the soul for Northern Ireland's political process' (11 October 2006).

In language reminiscent of their coverage of the Good Friday Agreement negotiations, the papers carried gloomy headlines about the progress of the talks and chances of final agreement. On successive days, the *Irish News* declared: 'Pressure on in Scotland but DUP digs in' (12 October 2006) and 'Governments prepare paper after Scotland talks hit a wall' (13 October 2006). The *News Letter* reported 'no sign of a breakthrough', with the DUP and Sinn Féin locked in 'a Mexican stand-off'; however it also referred to 'a flicker of a sign of progress in the evening after a day which had looked doomed' (13 October 2006). On Friday 13 October, an early edition of the *Belfast Telegraph* led with the news that, 'DUP reject shadow executive blueprint', a reference to a joint proposal on the table from the two governments that a shadow executive could operate while all other issues were being resolved. However, in its last edition of the day, the paper announced: 'Limited devolution deal within grasp'.

The Agreement

The St Andrews Agreement was in reality nothing more than a projected sequence of moves that the DUP and Sinn Féin had to choreograph towards the goal of a power-sharing government by 26 March 2007. This would start with Sinn Féin convening a special party conference (Ard Fheis) to seek support for the endorsement of policing.

The key theme that emerged in coverage of the final agreement was that of 'the road map', though the headlines and editorial assessments suggested that there might be different versions of the road map in circulation. The *News Letter*'s front page on 14 October pictured Ian Paisley and a headline quote that, 'Today we stand at a crossroads. There is a road to democracy and a road to anarchy'. An item inside by the paper's political editor was headed, 'Set fair – but a long way left to go'. The *Belfast Telegraph*, in its editorial, 'Rewards for those who take the hard road', thought the agreement was 'a clever construction [that] signposts the route to devolved government and the obstacles that have to be surmounted along the way'. The *Irish News* led on its front page with, 'Talks produce road map to revive peace process'. Its editorial, 'Agreement is step forward', described it as the culmination of 'an exceptionally long and difficult process [that] brought us within touching distance of a resolution'. The paper predicted that the parties would face other challenges along the way, 'but at long last events are moving in the right direction'.

Another aspect of this coverage is the way in which the unionist papers especially misinterpreted the British government's threats as policy rather than as a negotiating strategy. The government's public stance was that the restoration of devolution was the only chance the parties had to seize back control of policy on controversial issues such as academic selection and the reform of local government and public administration. The *News Letter* editorial – 'St Andrews may get us all out of the bunker' – referred to:

> the government's blind determination to introduce a rates system which is patently unfair and out of step with the rest of the UK, to push through changes to public administration structures without due consideration of local feelings and to press ahead with the scrapping of academic selection despite the opposition of the overwhelming majority of the people in the Province. (14 October 2006)

In a follow-up editorial on 16 October, the paper again referred to the government position, accusing the NIO of showing 'flagrant disregard for local opinion'. The *Belfast Telegraph* also urged the parties to respond positively to the Agreement, restore devolution and seize control of these policy issues.

Sending up the St Andrews talks

The coverage of the talks featured an element of satirical colour that contrasted sharply with the gravity that attended reporting of the Good Friday Agreement. This was a marker perhaps of growing exasperation with the seemingly interminable process. With the talks in apparent deadlock from the start, the *Belfast Telegraph* used the appearance of the movie actor, Bill Murray, days earlier at a nearby golf tournament, as a satirical reference point for an item headed, 'Groundhog Day at St Andrews – the Irish are coming to Scotland but will discussions be Lost in Translation?' (11 October 2006). It went on to reference other Bill Murray movies that seemed to sum up the farcical nature of yet more talks about talks on Northern Ireland's future, such as *Little Shop of Horrors* and *Ghostbusters*.

On Saturday 14 October, the paper's first edition led with the news that the people would have to go back to the polls to approve the new agreement, either in a new assembly election or a referendum. The headline, 'Back to the Future', framed a photomontage of Ian Paisley and Gerry Adams waving out of the sports car featured in the movie of the same name. A later edition dropped the story from the front page except for a photograph of a startled-looking Ian Paisley at the end-of-summit news conference, captioned with a mock quote: 'Surprise, surprise, we've got an agreement!' (14 October 2006).

The *Irish News* also indulged in some satire. Columnist, Tom Kelly, a former press officer at the NIO, imagined the agreement as the shotgun wedding of Ian Paisley and Gerry Adams under the headline, 'Unlikely union likely to be mother of all hooleys' (14 October 2006). Elsewhere in the same edition, an item setting out the detail of the agreement reflected on how the changing fortunes of the negotiations coincided with improvements in the weather at St Andrews. Headed, 'Outline of Agreement emerges from the mist', it ended with this footnote: 'The political talks opened in mist and rain on Wednesday with little optimism but concluded in the sunshine of blue skies yesterday amid hopes that the problems dogging the peace process are at last on the way to being finally resolved' (14 October 2006).

While we have so far demonstrated wholesale pro-Agreement consensus among the mainstream media, we think it important to show that there were alternative perspectives available, of which even a cursory reading would reveal the deep-seated suspicions and reservations that existed about the accord among grassroots republicanism and loyalism. We look now at the alternative print media available at the time of the Agreement, primarily those of republican and loyalists paramilitary organisations but also those offering socialist, feminist and humanist perspectives.

Alternative media perspectives

We identify three key differences between the mainstream media and the alternative press. The first is the way in which mainstream news focuses on contemporary events, while loyalist and republican newspapers have tended to contextualise these events within their long historical memories. The second is the way in which mainstream news concentrates on the role of political leaders and other key personnel in the political process, while the alternative press insists upon the centrality and agency of 'the people'. But the most glaring difference is that while mainstream news has been generally supportive of the peace process, the alternative press has been almost uniformly hostile to political negotiations and compromise, seeing it in the context of long histories of struggle, adversity and betrayal. Even the few that supported it, such as *An Phoblacht/Republican News*, had very different, politically antagonistic understandings as to what it meant.

Loyalist and republican perspectives

In Northern Ireland, journalists might find it convenient to ignore the historical context when there is no agreed or taken-for-granted version of the past. Arguably, the interpretation of the mainstream press of the Agreement as a new beginning implies a break with the divisive past. The alternative press, on the other hand, is less inclined to move on. It makes liberal reference to history by way of offering its readers a framework within which to understand the present. It also pays particular attention to the role of the 'people' in history, who are invariably represented as stoic or suffering, qualities that help to distinguish them from their treacherous political leaders. Of course, the various histories recalled in the alternative press are contentious, serving the present political needs of their publishers. They nevertheless offer a crucial contrast with how mainstream news interprets and represents the political process. While commercial and public service news look for 'progress', loyalist and republican newspapers are more concerned with historical continuity.

In this respect, *An Phoblacht/Republican News* was careful to reassure its readers that, despite the new peace accord, the future would be sufficiently like the past and this was reason for optimism. Throughout the spring and summer of 1998, the paper reflected this optimism in a series of upbeat headlines: 'Forward in struggle' (23 April 1998); 'United we stand' (7 May 1998); 'The struggle continues' (14 May 1998); and 'Looking to the future' (21 May 1998). Two of these front pages featured photographs of leading republicans before the Sinn Féin Ard Fheis (party conference) posing with clenched-fist salutes. The message was one of republican unity and continued defiance in the new dispensation. The armalite may have given way to the ballot box but *An Phoblacht/Republican News* was keen to impress upon its readers continuity with the past and confidence in the future. Readers could be assured that even if republican tactics had changed, the struggle continued. In this way *An Phoblacht/Republican News* combined historical continuity with an affirmative vision of the future.

Other republican papers were scathing in their assessment of the Sinn Féin leadership's participation in the peace process and, by association, *An Phoblacht/Republican News*. They saw history as a yardstick by which the republican leadership's deviance from principle was measured. *Sovereign Nation* remarked on the 'irony' of Sinn Féin leaders signing up to a document that fell short of republican goals in the year of the bicentenary of the United Irish uprising (summer 1998). *Saoirse* accused Sinn Féin of being the 'latest "spare wheel" to be pressed into service by the British Crown', standing in a succession of other nationalist parties that had betrayed the cause of Irish freedom (May 1998). This concept of history as a series of betrayals figured keenly in *Saoirse*'s response to the Agreement, and it was attended by a tremendous sense of persecution: 'The Irish people have been denied peace for 829 years, since 1169AD in fact. We have suffered invasion, confiscation, plantation and famine, as England illegally seized our country and exploited our people'. The article concluded with a bleak projection of the future: 'How many more generations must endure agony, because some people have not the courage to confront the basic problem?' (May 1998). For *Saoirse*, Sinn Féin had run away from the problem and left the 'Irish people' to their historic suffering.

A sense of historical betrayal also marked the response of loyalist publications. *Leading the Way*, the journal associated with the Loyalist Volunteer Force, referred to the unionist leaders that had negotiated and signed the Agreement as 'Lundies'. The term 'Lundies' can only have been used to arouse the popular memory of Colonel Robert Lundy, the Governor of Derry, who stood accused of treachery for his readiness to surrender Derry in 1688 to the forces of the Catholic King James II. When *Leading the Way* recalled Lundy it served as historical shorthand, associating the contemporary unionist leadership with his supposed treachery. Seen in these terms the Agreement was 'a conspiracy to fool the Unionist people and lead them down the slippery slope into Irish Unity'. According to *Leading the Way*, political leaders were duping the 'brave citizens of Ulster' (May 1998).

Similarly, the loyalist journal *Warrior* combined historical myth and disaffection with political figureheads. The unionist parties, *Warrior* explained, were 'useless bastards', 'cowards' and 'lackeys' that had rendered 'the Ulster people, the most maligned, marginalised, and attacked people in western Europe'. To remedy this dire situation, *Warrior* argued that loyalists had to recognise their seemingly prehistoric claim to the Ulster 'motherland': 'It is the country which for three centuries, since the rebirth of our nation, has been our home. We have no other home. This is our land and through our history we are bound to it' (June 1998).

The *Orange Standard*, the monthly paper of the Orange Order, was more temperate in its language and respectful of the unionist establishment when it asked its readers to reject the Good Friday Agreement. Nevertheless, keeping faith with the past was a crucial way of legitimising the convictions of rejectionist loyalism. The front page of the *Standard*'s May 1998 edition was emphatic in its rejection of the Agreement. Under the simple headline, 'No', it implored 'pro-Union voters to have the courage of their convictions and, with the belief in protecting their birthright and heritage [and] do what is right for their beloved province'. Typically the *Orange Standard* carried within its pages a dire warning of the 'treachery of perfidious Albion', claiming that it would suit 'the selfish interests of many in modern Britain if loyal Ulster were sacrificed on the altar of expediency' (May 1998). Another contributor reflected on the historical significance of the referendum, arguing that it 'could be the most important decision we [Orangemen] have collectively taken as a group in 400 years of Ulster-Scots history' (McDowell 1998).

Alone among the loyalist publications, *Combat*, associated with the Ulster Volunteer Force (UVF), combined support for the Good Friday Agreement with a call to break with the past on some level. 'The opportunity for change is within our grasp,' it claimed, 'to ensure a brighter, better, safer future for all'. It dwelt less on ideas of heritage and presented the past as one of ignominy, arguing that 'to keep wallowing in the past could mean a return to the bloodshed of the past on a scale that would be too horrific to contemplate'. Yet even while it recommended the Agreement, *Combat* was not immune to expressing dissatisfaction with unionist leaders. It accused them of having 'ranted and raved' ineffectually in the face of the republican threat to Northern Ireland at the start of the troubles. Typically, in contrast to their leaders' ineptitude, 'the people moved to defend themselves, and so the Loyalist paramilitaries came into being' (May 2008).

Socialist, feminist and humanist perspectives

Just as loyalist and republican journals were divided in their various responses to the Agreement, there was also little consensus among some of the smaller political and social constituencies in Northern Ireland. Most socialist publications, all of which are produced by one or other of the small left organisations that exist in Northern Ireland, viewed the accord as having the potential further to entrench sectarianism by providing for power-sharing between unionists and nationalists. However these publications differed in their strategic and tactical responses. The *Socialist Voice*, the monthly paper of the Socialist Party in Ireland, welcomed the Agreement only in so far as it provided an opportunity for an alternative, 'based on the common interests of working people', its equivocal position clear in the front-page headline 'No to bigots, yes to class politics' (May 1998). The *Socialist Worker*, the fortnightly paper of the Socialist Workers Party in Ireland, rejected the Agreement outright as a 'boss's deal, designed only to institutionalise sectarianism in the interests of the right wing party who negotiated it' (18–31 April 1998). Only the Communist Party of Ireland's weekly, *Unity*, offered an affirmative assessment of the Agreement, seeing in it the basis for an end to violence, sectarianism and development of working class politics (25 April 1998). Other publications such as the feminist *Women's News* and the *Ulster Humanist* took no editorial stand on the Agreement. *Women's News* asked in a headline 'If the Agreement is voted in, is it a good thing for women?' and printed a list of unattributed responses, most of which looked favourably on the accord; some were sceptical, others were rejectionist and one professed no knowledge that there even was an Agreement (May–June 1998). Where *Women's News* strove for inclusivity, the *Ulster Humanist* looked for balance by offering two different humanist perspectives on the Agreement; one advocating a yes vote in the name of compromise and the 'Middle Way', the other suspicious that sectarianism and violence would be institutionalised under the terms of the Agreement (May–June 1998). The Agreement posed a challenge then to the politics of constituencies beyond unionism and nationalism, with some seeing it as an opportunity to advance their own causes, while others worried that it would simply further embed sectarianism in the political culture of Northern Ireland, a setback therefore to their own ambitions.

Implications of coverage

The mainstream, local media lent significant support to the Good Friday Agreement and a Yes vote in the referendum, taking cues from Prime Minister Tony Blair's talk of 'the hand of history', 'no alternatives' and the 'eyes of the civilised world'. Of the three daily newspapers, the *News Letter* was the most emphatic in its promotion of Blair's message but all three papers acclaimed the positive overall Yes vote as marking a promising new era for Northern Ireland and downplayed the implications of the less than decisive, 50-50 vote among the unionist electorate that voted. Given that the *Belfast Telegraph* and the *News Letter* are regarded as unionist in terms of content and editorial stance, this stands as something of a serious editorial misjudgement because the ambivalent unionist support for the Agreement would become a decisive factor in how the political process unfolded over the following decade.

Two developments in particular turned the initial heady optimism about the future, post-Good Friday Agreement, into gloomy pessimism that the peace process had run aground. Firstly, the new Northern Ireland Assembly and Executive, elected and constituted in July 1998, limped from crisis to crisis until finally collapsing into suspension in 2002. Secondly, the DUP and Sinn Féin, long thought of as parties on opposite extremes of the political divide, emerged through a series of elections in this period – to the new Northern Ireland Assembly and to Westminster – as the leading representatives of unionism and nationalism respectively. Sinn Féin's cause was helped considerably by the final and complete act of IRA decommissioning in September 2005, removing from the table one of the most critical unionist objections to sharing power with the party.

All this came as a shock to the liberal, political establishment, especially to so-called moderate unionism and nationalism. It was not how the Good Friday Agreement was supposed to work out, yet a realistic analysis would suggest that real agreement between unionism and nationalism in Northern Ireland could never have been achieved without the DUP and Sinn Féin moving into the centre-ground and bringing their sizeable constituencies with them. In truth, the construction of 'moderate unionism and nationalism' as represented by the UUP and the SDLP had served its ideological, hegemonic purpose through the decades of conflict in Northern Ireland, more as the politics of containment than as a progressive politics that would hold the key to real and profound conflict resolution. The British and Irish governments, the architects of the Good Friday Agreement, failed to recognise this and marginalised rather than accommodated those more inclined to say No than Yes to the founding principles of the settlement they proposed. In this context, the repeated photo opportunities of Trimble shaking hands with Hume, usually overseen by Tony Blair, copper-fastened the central misapprehension of the Agreement. It was a mistake, therefore, for Tony Blair to ignore the opposition to the Good Friday Agreement and certainly an inexcusable error for a newspaper such as the *Belfast Telegraph* to praise David Trimble for the way he deployed 'logic in the face of the emotional arguments put forward by the No campaign' (23 May 1998).

This is why it is important, we think, to consider alternative media perspectives where they exist. While these are as open to scholarly critique as the mainstream media they, at the very least, offered a range of alternative, sometimes genuinely constructive viewpoints on the Agreement that were marginalised or dismissed by the mainstream newspapers. It seems obvious now to state that republican and loyalist publications in particular represented the views of armed groups whose consent to political settlement was crucial if the Agreement were to have any chance of working in the long term. Yet their objections and anxieties and those of other dissident voices failed to gain any traction on the slippery terrain of centre-ground politics.

Notes

1. Audit Bureau of Circulations UK (2009), http://www.abc.org.uk. Accessed September 2009. For a detailed survey of the local media market in Northern Ireland, see McLaughlin 2006.
2. Journalism has been called the first draft of history yet if one consults some of the recent histories and journalistic memoirs of the Agreement, it soon becomes clear that it will be some time yet before we get a close-to-accurate understanding of how the Agreement was reached around those critical few days inside government buildings (see the varying accounts by, for example: Hennessey 2000; MacGinty and Darby 2002; Maille and McKittrick 1996; McKittrick 1996; Mitchell 1999; O'Clery 1996; Purdy 2005).

Chapter 3

Public History and the Peace Process

In the previous chapter we saw how Northern Ireland's local newspapers were unequivocal in their support for the Good Friday Agreement and greeted its achievement as an occasion of epic historical significance. It was somewhat serendipitous then that the Agreement coincided with the bicentenary of the United Irish rebellion because the ambitions of Irish patriots in 1798 provided a tragic antecedent to the potentially epic feat of the peace process.

Moderates and liberals in Northern Ireland had long venerated the United Irish aspiration to unite Protestant, Catholic and Dissenter so for them the peace process promised some sort of comparable cross-community accord. Indeed, the resonance of the United Irishmen's ambition was felt beyond this historically beleaguered liberal constituency, reaching sections that have traditionally been hostile to the legacy of 1798. Republicans could be relied upon to mark the anniversary of the rebellion each year but this time there were other commemorations that emanated from some surprising sources, such as unionist-dominated councils.

Such plurality was integral to the most important commemorative exhibition of the United Irishmen that year at the Ulster Museum. Entitled *Up in Arms*, it offered an impeccably liberal account of the period, apparent in its foregrounding of the United Irish aspiration to 'a cordial union among all the people of Ireland' (Ulster Museum, *Up in Arms exhibition guide* 1998: 1). But it was a selective history and it required the Ulster Museum to downplay the movement's stated separatist ambitions in favour of a version of the past that sat more comfortably with the 'official' preference for an 'agreed Ireland', as expressed in the Downing Street Declaration of 1993. Essentially, the United Irishmen were being pressed into the ideological service of contemporary 'official' and liberal ambitions.

Nevertheless, liberal pluralist interpretations of the past and 'official' attempts to underscore them have not gone unchallenged, for despite the present political settlement there is no consensus about the past and both unionists and nationalists continue to define themselves with reference to antagonistic histories. This means that any public display about the past that offers some perceived slight or offence to one side or the other is unlikely to go unchallenged.[1] In an atmosphere of such antagonism, institutions charged with the responsibility of displaying history for public consumption have traditionally trod carefully.

This chapter looks in particular at the strategies adopted by the Ulster Museum; the closest Northern Ireland has to what might be called a 'national' museum. Its initial response to the sectarian character of the society around it was a prolonged period of quietism on most aspects of Ireland's political history. This lasted until the 1990s when the changing political climate provided the context for two major exhibitions, *Kings in Conflict* and *Up in Arms*; the former marking the tercentenary of the Battle of the Boyne in 1690; the latter, the bicentenary of the United Irish uprising in 1798. Both were didactic exhibitions, typical of the representational strategies of the modern 'national' museum. However, in a more recent exhibition that opened in 2004, the authoritative voice of the museum was harder to discern. *Conflict: the Irish at War*, a history of conflict in Ireland from the Mesolithic period (7000–4500 BC) until the present, demonstrated an apparent willingness to incorporate the reflections and responses of selected members of the public in a manner that might be said to offer a privatised or personalised view of the past.

Despite its initial policy of quietism, the Ulster Museum assumed itself a British institution until political developments prompted a more considered approach to Ireland's political history. To avoid controversy, exhibitions such as *Kings in Conflict* and *Up in Arms* viewed local events within a broad European and international context. This had the welcome effect of challenging the historical myopia and particularism of Ulster unionism and Irish nationalism but it also gave the museum the appearance of being 'above it all', while denying its own bourgeois and liberal sensibilities. However, liberal representations of the past are hard to sustain in an environment where sectarian and diametrically opposing political views hold sway. In this context the subjective approach of *Conflict: the Irish at War* is in keeping with the present political settlement in Northern Ireland and in step with 'new museological' strategies that have challenged the old didactic museum form. Nevertheless, this new approach can be accused of an historical relativism that risks leaving intact sectarian histories, whereas the didactic liberalism of previous exhibitions at least had the virtue of offering some sort of challenge, however piecemeal, to unionism and nationalism. Also, in the personal responses of its contributors to historical artifacts there is a case to be answered that the museum offers a subjective version of the past that reneges on the very idea of history.

Museums, nation and class

The initial reluctance of the Ulster Museum to engage in any sustained or meaningful way with the political history of Ireland is explicable given the country's divided national allegiances and its history of colonialism and conflict. Such a history and politics sit uneasily with the modern museum form that, throughout the nineteenth century, developed as an expression of bourgeois confidence and an important apparatus through which to imagine the nation at a time of imperial expansion and capitalist development. In the museum, national achievements were celebrated and could be contrasted with the exotic artifacts of primitive and subjugated Others. As Sharon J. MacDonald explains, museums articulated 'two temporal narratives: one, a distinctive national trajectory and, two, the nation as final triumphant stage of successive progression' (MacDonald 2003: 3). She also identifies a third narrative, 'the immemorial', inspired by the classical design of museum buildings in the nineteenth century, 'implying age and continuity through time' (MacDonald 2003: 3).

As well as their specific national contexts, museums have had an important class dimension. They represented the order that the bourgeoisie presumed it had imposed on the world in terms of scientific, technological and social progress. Eric Hobsbawm has argued that bourgeois society in the mid- to late-1800s had a 'secular ideology of progress' (Hobsbawm 1975: 271) that considered history a process of continuous social improvement and advancement. Society had at this time:

> no serious doubts about the direction in which [it] was going and ought to go, and the methods, intellectual or practical, of getting there. Nobody doubted the fact of progress, both material and intellectual, since it seemed too obvious to be denied. (Hobsbawm 1975: 253).

Museums were precisely one of the sites where that progress appeared obvious and difficult to refute. Objects and artifacts were displayed within the apparently unmediated context of the glass case, which seemed to allow them to 'speak for themselves', vouching for the objectivity and realism of the museum form. In truth, museum exhibitions were processes of selection, classification and organisation, all requiring human intervention. Indeed, the meta-narrative of progress that museums propagated was supported by imposing a linear, chronological arrangement upon historical artifacts. Such linearity emphasised continuity over contradiction, and combined with the assumption of objectivity offered a seemingly coherent, unified and objective position from which to view the past. Crucially for the museum's bourgeois patrons, they were offered an historical perspective that confirmed their contemporary legitimacy and superiority. Museums then, as Bennett argues, became the 'machinery for producing progressivist subjects' (Bennett 1995: 47).

This basic form of representing the past in museums remained pretty much unaltered throughout the twentieth century and it is only recently that it has come under scrutiny from a 'new museology' (Vergo 1989). It has underpinned the exhibition strategies of the Ulster Museum despite the identifiable problems the institution faced producing 'progressivist subjects' in the context of the north of Ireland, where national validation and the explicit celebration of imperial achievement were more problematic and potentially controversial. This is not to say though that the Ulster Museum was politically benign.

Quietism and 'serving the whole of Northern Ireland'

In 1979 the then director of the Ulster Museum, W. A. McCutcheon, emphasised the institution's modern credentials and national context, situating it firmly within 'the social and cultural history of an expanding industrial and commercial city' and ranking it among the 'main museums in Great Britain outside London' (Nesbitt 1979). Indeed the museum assumed its position within Great Britain by demonstrating its commitment to a British master narrative. Just two years before McCutcheon's comments the museum staged an exhibition to coincide with and celebrate the Silver Jubilee in 1977. Before that, in 1964, there had been a commemoration of the outbreak of the two world wars and an exhibition in 1966 marking the fiftieth anniversary of the Battle of the Somme. The Somme in particular holds a crucial, emblematic position within unionism's popular memory. Casualties sustained by the 36th Division (predominantly made up of Edward Carson's Ulster Volunteer Force) were seen in unionism's eyes to legitimise Northern Ireland's Britishness.

It is difficult to believe then, as McCutcheon did in 1979, that the Ulster Museum was a national institution that served the 'whole of Northern Ireland'. Rather its assumption of Northern Ireland's Britishness was possible only by ignoring Irish nationalist perspectives. This strategy was aided by the absence of exhibitions or commemorations that addressed in any direct way the political controversies of Ireland's past. Yet the Ulster Museum's quietism on this point was not untypical of museum policy throughout Northern Ireland at the time. Not only was there a relative absence of museums compared with the rest of the UK (Crooke 2001: 124), but also caution was bred into their formation. This was apparent in a statement by a previous director of the Museums' Council when he described Northern Ireland as 'a very divided and traditional society [that] viewed the examination of history as potentially divisive' (Aidan Walsh, quoted in Crooke 2001: 125).

Kings in Conflict: tackling the 'insular view'

Quietism and caution were the norm until 1990 when the Ulster Museum produced a major exhibition to accompany the tercentenary of the Battle of the Boyne, a date that holds particular significance for Ulster loyalism. The victory of William of Orange over James II in 1690 secured the Protestant ascendancy in Ireland and is celebrated annually by Ulster loyalists on 12 July. As such, any commemoration of the period has the potential to alienate nationalists. The *Kings in Conflict* exhibition attempted to avoid this by striving for impeccable sectarian balance and by presenting the conflict within a broad European context. The then director of the Museum, J. C. Nolan, wrote in the preface to the exhibition's catalogue that:

> Folk memory has emphasised the conflict as one between two rival kings, William III and James II, in contention for the throne of England. Gaelic Ireland referred to it as Cogadh an Dá Rí – the War of the Two Kings – reflecting a somewhat insular view. (Ulster Museum 1990: vii)

To counter such insularity the kings referred to in the exhibition's title include Louis XIV of France as well as William III and James II. The point is emphasised in the promotional material and literature that accompanied the exhibition and that included portraits of the three European monarchs.

The Museum's new-found willingness to engage with some of the more contentious aspects of Ireland's history corresponded with developments in the political process. In November 1985, the British and Irish Governments signed the Anglo-Irish Agreement, which provided Dublin with a consultative role in the government of Northern Ireland. Its ostensible objective was to foster peace and reconciliation but only caused unionist outrage, thus achieving little by way of better community relations. However the Anglo-Irish Agreement was also an attempt to head off the political advance of Sinn Féin, which had scored a considerable propaganda victory and electoral success on the back of the republican hunger strikes in 1981. By June 1983, the Sinn Féin vote was 13.4%, an indication that they were gaining on the constitutional nationalists, the Social Democratic and Labour Party (SDLP) on 17.9%. One of the key objectives for both London and Dublin was to shore up nationalist support for the SDLP and this required the Anglo-Irish Agreement to address the alienation felt by nationalists in the North of Ireland. Among the measures taken to redress nationalist grievances were the introduction of fair employment legislation, closer checks on controversial loyalist parades and the repeal of the Flags and Emblems (Display) Act (Northern Ireland) 1954 that discriminated against nationalist symbols in public places. In this new political climate, the Ulster Museum could not assume that exhibitions commemorating British achievements would 'serve the whole of Northern Ireland' (W. A. McCutcheon, quoted in Nesbitt 1997).

Kings in Conflict opened in 1990 just as a new political initiative was afoot. In November that year, the recently appointed Secretary of State for Northern Ireland, Peter Brooke, made a speech stating that the British government had 'no selfish strategic or economic interest in Northern Ireland'[2]. An advanced copy of Brooke's speech was forwarded to Sinn Féin as part of the re-instigation of the secret line of communication between republicans and the British administration, an indication of the British government's new thinking.

Brooke's remarks were reiterated in the Downing Street Declaration 1993, which also stated that the British government's 'primary interest is to see peace, stability and reconciliation established by agreement among all the people who inhabit the island of Ireland'[3]. Crucial here is the word 'agreement'. Used liberally throughout the document, the language of an agreed Ireland had been adopted from the phraseology of the Hume-Adams negotiations of the early 1990s, yet despite these nationalist origins it took on a calculated ambiguity once appropriated by the 'official' discourse of the Downing Street Declaration (and later, much of the Good Friday Agreement). This is because it needed to have the capacity to facilitate the polarised expectations of unionism and nationalism.

Up in Arms and an 'agreed Ireland'

For the Ulster Museum, the notion of an 'agreed Ireland' presented it with the opportunity in the *Up in Arms* exhibition to offer a rhetorical and political antecedent to the contemporary official discourse. The preface to the exhibition guide set the tone:

The rebellion which broke out in Ireland in 1798 would turn out to be the bloodiest in Ireland's turbulent history. Between 20,000 and 30,000 people were killed during the summer months of that year. And yet, only a few years earlier, it had all appeared so promising. The United Irishmen, who instigated the uprising, had in 1791 called for 'a cordial union among all the people of Ireland'. The exhibition presents over 300 sources, many obtained from other museums, which outline the circumstances in which that hope turned to tragedy (Ulster Museum, *Up in Arms exhibition guide* 1998: 1).

The United Irishmen's aspiration to 'a cordial union among all the people of Ireland' was analogous with the 'official' preference for an agreed Ireland but ambiguous enough to avoid controversial political commitments, either of the unionist or nationalist variety. Crucially, the aspiration to 'a cordial union' sat comfortably with the ideology of the Community Relations Council (CRC), which directed funds from the European Union's Special Support Programme for Peace and Reconciliation to sponsor the *Up in Arms* exhibition.

The CRC was set up by the British government in 1990 as an independent organisation to promote better community relations through the recognition of a 'shared discourse which recognises and affirms differences'.[4] The other sponsors of *Up in Arms* were the unionist Belfast *Newsletter* and the nationalist *Irish News* as well as the Belfast City Council, underlining the Museum's commitment to strive for an 'agreed' or 'shared discourse'.

In keeping with this objective, *Up in Arms* presented a history in which no one was very much to blame. Of course, the Ulster Museum could do little to indict sectarianism, since 'respect' for sectarian differences was inscribed in the 'official' view that it adopted. So, in the exhibition's accompanying literature the United Irish leadership was accused of naiveté[5] and disorganisation[6]; attention was drawn to oppressive English security measures[7]; the Irish Parliament, bastion of ascendancy power, was charged with corruption[8]; and while sectarianism was implicated in the defeat of liberal ambitions, the proponents of that sectarianism were never charged in the *Up in Arms* exhibition.[9] For instance, Orange Order paraphernalia from the period was displayed but never interrogated for its sectarian significance. Instead, objects such as a folding wall chart belonging to the 1st Loyal Orange Boyne Society from 1798 that was used in the initiation of new members to the society, was described as a 'remarkable item' (Ulster Museum, *Up in Arms catalogue* 1998: 140). Why it was remarkable was never made clear but its place in the Museum might be said to bestow upon the object an aesthetic and historic value that transcended the sectarianism of its original conception.

If no one was utterly to blame for 1798, everyone apparently shared in its tragedy. The preface of the *Up in Arms catalogue* closes thus: 'Catholic and Dissenter rebels experienced the bitterness of defeat, the Protestant Ascendancy saved their property but lost the "independence" they had gained in 1782, sectarian divisions were sharpened rather than assuaged' (Ulster Museum, *Up in Arms catalogue* 1998: 1).

This is not just the tragedy of a massive loss of human life. For the Ulster Museum it was a political tragedy because it denied the institution a national history that could facilitate the sort of progressivist narrative museums traditionally exalt. As Raymond Williams points out, the 'successful revolution, we might say, becomes not tragedy but epic' when it is remembered as 'the origin of a people' and as such considered 'a necessary condition of life' (Williams 1966: 64). However, 1798 is not 'the origin of a people' but as *Up in Arms* proposes 'the seed-bed of both unionism and republican nationalism' (Ulster Museum, *Up in Arms catalogue* 1998: 1). In essence it is the period when linearity and objectivity, the representational strategies that underpin narratives of national achievement and progress in the modern museum form, become unsustainable in the face of diametrically opposing political points of view. That is at least until the 1990s when the commitment to an 'agreed Ireland' provided a potentially unified subject position from which the 'progressivist subject' can view Ireland's tragic past.

Contesting form and content

Museums might be said to *materialise* the past through the objects and artifacts that make up their exhibitions. This means that museums tend to skew history in ways that privilege the rich because they tend to leave a more substantial cultural and material trace of their existence. *Up in Arms* was overwhelmingly composed of artifacts and objects pertaining to the bourgeoisie and ascendancy in Ireland, and the governing classes of eighteenth-century Britain. The *objets d'art*, paintings and paraphernalia of the ascendancy were spectacular. These included commanding portraits of the Earl of Harcourt, lord lieutenant of Ireland from 1772 to 1776, Arthur Chichester, 5th Earl of Donegal, James Stewart of Killymoon, MP for County Tyrone in the Irish Parliament and John Reilly, MP of Scarvagh. The smallest of these portraits was an impressive 123cm x 99cm.

Up in Arms also included a 'Man's suit of satin with floral embroidery, c. 1775–80', accompanied by an 'Open robe and petticoat of ivory raised and figured silk with brocaded flowers, and ribbons and leaves of gold thread' (Ulster Museum, *Up in Arms catalogue* 1998: 24). This was in a section of the exhibition dedicated to the Protestant ascendancy, the centrepiece of which was a 28-piece silver toilet service, commissioned by Robert Fitzgerald, nineteenth Earl of Kildare, as a gift to his wife. All these objects ably represented the opulence of the Anglo-Irish aristocracy, while their political power was demonstrated in exhibits such as the suit and staff of Black Rod of Ireland; Francis Wheatley's painting of the Irish Commons in 1780; the regalia of the Most Illustrious Order of St Patrick; and the title pages of the Acts of the Irish Parliament that brought into effect the Penal Laws.

The rising international bourgeoisie of the period was also represented by a variety of portraits. These tend to be more modest paintings than those of their aristocratic counterparts, though they are still impressive. Benjamin Franklin reading his correspondence at a table bedecked with books; George Washington, statesman-like, pictured again at a table, surrounded by books and a bill or letter at his hand; and Thomas Paine, holding before him his two major contributions to political thought, *Common Sense* (1776) and *Rights of*

Man (1791). These portraits indicate statesmanship, industry, scholarship and literacy. They stand in sharp contrast to those of the aristocratic ascendancy in Ireland, whose pictures emphasise leisure, military prowess and divine authority. The aristocratic milieu was evident in the reproduction of Viscount Castlereagh with a golf club. The *Up in Arms catalogue* tells us helpfully that this is 'almost certainly the first known illustration of an Irish golfer' (Ulster Museum, *Up in Arms catalogue* 1998: 31). The 5th Earl of Donegal was also shown relaxing on his estate, while the Earl of Harcourt posed in his robes of office, signifying his conferred authority, and with a sword at his side serving as a sign of how that authority is maintained.

The artifacts and objects left by the affluent sections of Irish and British society in the period are splendid and lavish demonstrations of political might and cultural acumen. In an exhibition of such ostentatious and opulent artifacts, how could exhibit number 296, the death mask of a Templepatrick weaver, Jemmy Hope, compete for attention? In *Up in Arms*, the materials pertaining to the working people of the eighteenth Century were dwarfed both numerically and aesthetically by those of the prosperous. Hence, the political and social contributions of working people in that period were under-represented and history in *Up in Arms* was skewed in favour of the elite classes. In this respect, John Gray's commemorative pamphlet, *The Sans Culottes of Belfast* (Gray 1998), offered an important alternative perspective on 1798 from that of *Up in Arms*.

Calling upon other facts from those privileged in the Ulster Museum, Gray recalls the contributions of men like Jemmy Hope in the 1798 uprising, as well as charting the tensions within the radical movement in Belfast at that time, between the distinct classes and class factions that made up the United Irishmen. *The Sans Culottes of Belfast* examines the radicalisation of 'the men of no property', their struggle with their bourgeois masters and their efforts to have their demands included in the revolutionary programme of the era. If *Up in Arms* is a centrist account of 1798, then John Gray offers a perspective from the margins. Significantly, the primary sources for *The Sans Culottes of Belfast* are two bourgeois newspapers of the time, the radical *Northern Star* and the less radical, though liberal, *News Letter*. There is an important point to be made here about the dependence of orthodox history on documentary and material evidence. Gray relies upon a symptomatic reading of Belfast's bourgeois press to piece together the story of working people in the city. This is necessarily so because of the relative paucity of documents and materials directly attributable to the lower classes.

Gray's account of 1798 was not the only alternative to the Ulster Museum's liberal history. Dissident republicans clearly rejected the consensual emphasis placed on the idea of a 'cordial union' by the museum and instead highlighted the United Irish movement's separatist ambitions. In her Bodenstown address, the vice-president of Republican Sinn Féin, Mary Ward, used the occasion of the bicentenary celebrations to assert the claim of anti-Agreement republicanism to the United Irishmen's legacy, berating Provisional Sinn Féin, the SDLP and, significantly, revisionist historians, all of whom she accused of omitting 'the (Wolfe) Tone dictat "to break the connection with England"'.[10] The Orange Order also struck a dissenting note and responded to the bicentenary by reprinting *Murder Without Sin*, an extract from Robert Ogle Gowan's book, *Orangeism, Its Origins and History*, first published in 1859. This re-publication of a text that is more than one hundred years old seemed to signal that the Orange institution's historiography of the events of that period had not moved on in that time.

The Orange Order posed a more serious challenge to the political accord in 1998, for just as Ulster Museum was marking the bicentenary of the United Irish uprising, loyalists were engaged in widespread violent protests, sparked by the banning of an Orange parade commemorating the Battle of the Somme from the Garvaghy Road in Portadown. The sharp contrast between loyalist street demonstrations and the institutional and contemplative atmosphere of the Ulster Museum brought into acute focus another problem surrounding the public exhibition and commemoration of history in Northern Ireland. Not only is the content of history potentially divisive, the form that its commemoration and exhibition takes can also be controversial and raises questions about public behaviour on such occasions.

As Tony Bennett argues, the nineteenth-century museum strove not only for intellectual improvement among its patrons but also provided lessons in civic conduct, aiming to produce a citizenry that would 'monitor and regulate its own behaviour' (Bennett 1995: 8) while at the same time acquiring 'a degree of corporate self-consciousness' (Bennett 1995: 25). In short, museums were conceived of as part of a bourgeois public sphere through which civilised and decorous behaviour would be promulgated; in which the rising middle class could present and come to know itself; and to which the unruly working class could be exposed in ways that might make them more acceptable to bourgeois company. The museum in Belfast was an exponent of these values and strategies almost from its inception. In 1845 the museum opened on the Easter Monday holiday to facilitate and encourage working-class attendance. Afterwards organisers noted, with a sense of barely concealed relief, that 'the utmost decorum and quietness was observed, no object in the collections being damaged' (Nesbitt 1979: 13). Unquestionably this was a policy aimed at offering an alternative to the bawdy and boozy temptations of a public holiday and a way of channelling working-class energies away from disorderly behaviour and 'low' habits. Significantly, it is around this time that informal working-class leisure pursuits in Belfast became increasingly formalised. The excesses of unregulated popular culture were gradually channelled into institutional forms – theatre, music hall etc – where public behaviour could be subject to greater regulation (Jackson 1995: 345).

Clearly cognisant of the potentially 'civilising' influence that public institutions can play, the British government's response to the loyalist street protests in 1998 was to offer to fund an Orange heritage centre if the loyalists would waive their claim to parade on the Garvaghy Road.[11] However, the offer was rejected. A heritage centre presumably held little attraction for an organisation whose roots lie in the eighteenth-century forms of popular assembly that constituted the low-Other of the bourgeois public sphere. Perhaps Orangemen were not yet ready to see their 'living tradition' reduced to a sanitised nostalgia or ersatz heritage.

Despite opposition from large sections of loyalism and dissident republicans to the new political dispensation, commemorations of 1798 were largely affirmative. As well as *Up in Arms* at the Ulster Museum, the Down County Museums held an exhibition and conference to mark the bicentenary; Lisburn's Irish Linen Centre and Museum also produced an exhibition; the Ards Borough Council held lectures, tours and re-enactments; and Newtownabbey Borough Council provided a comprehensive programme of events from early May until late June. There were also numerous historical and commemorative pamphlets and books, and both BBC Northern Ireland and UTV found ways in which to mark the bicentenary. The United Irishmen had not always provided the means to affirm a shared heritage. Commemorative acts at the time of the centenary were marred by ugly clashes between nationalists and unionists. That unionist-dominated councils such as Ards, Lisburn and Newtownabbey could mark the United Irish uprising one hundred years later was testament to some significant change in the political atmosphere. Nevertheless, the exhibition of Northern Ireland's recent past remains more problematic than that of Ireland two hundred years ago.

The Tower Museum in Derry has come up with a novel way of compensating for political divisions by offering a bi-linear narrative consisting of unionist and nationalist versions of the past from 1880 onwards. Separate unionist and nationalist histories, and the artifacts pertaining to them, are displayed down either side of a simulated road. As Desmond Bell has argued, this offers a preferred and privileged viewing position where the visitor is 'literally invited to occupy the middle of the road in a terrain clearly seen as contested' (Bell 1998: 250).

Conflict: the Irish at War and personalising the past

The Ulster Museum appeared to have abandoned history altogether in its exhibition, *Conflict: the Irish at War* (December 2003). This exhibition included artifacts pertaining to Northern Ireland's recent troubled past carefully situated in the context of a long history of conflict beginning with the Mesolithic period (7000–4500BC). As a consequence of this, conflict in Ireland is configured almost entirely in endogenous terms. The durability of violence is apparent in the 10,000 years covered by the exhibition, giving the impression that Ireland is a place of interminable violence. Both the endogenous explanation of the 'troubles' and the notion that the Irish are a race apart, genetically predisposed to conflict, have long provided ideological cover for the British State and its claim that it is somehow a neutral arbiter in the conflict.

The other crucial distinction between *Conflict* and its predecessors was its inclusion of a range of 'voices' drawn from a cross-section of people who, as the exhibition guide explains, were asked to comment on the objects that 'reflected their own experience of or views on conflict and warfare' (Ulster Museum 2003: 44). These were available on mobile handsets and while their use seemed to forgo the authoritative tones of the institution, the contributors were not self-selecting but appointed by the Museum. It nevertheless indicated a shift in perspective on the past, from the assumed objectivity of *Kings in Conflict* and *Up in Arms* to subjective positions. This was further emphasised by the inclusion of a 'rest and study' area where visitors were invited to contemplate the exhibition – read books that had been provided, watch film clips or listen to recordings from *Legacy*, a BBC Radio Ulster series in which 'ordinary people' reflected on their experience of the 'troubles'; patrons were even invited to write a poem and enter it in a competition. Subjective views of the past might be seen as a move away from the didactic museum exhibition towards a more democratic and inclusive view of the past. On the other hand, the plurality of 'voices' might just as easily be considered a way of avoiding any genuine effort to interpret and explain the past where it is so vociferously disputed and open to sectarian interpretation.

There are other forces at work besides sectarianism that might be thought of as underscoring the diminution of public history in Ireland. David Brett has investigated the rise of heritage, seeing it as 'a product of the process of modernisation which, by eroding customs and expectations, forces us to re-articulate our sense of the past' (Brett 1996: 8). He concludes that heritage 'holds out the false promise that something can be preserved that will not melt away in air' (Brett 1996: 158). Brett's analysis implies a 'nostalgic subject' at odds with the present. On the other hand, it is a 'consumerist subject' that emerges in what Roy Foster sees as 'theme park reconstructions and soundbite-sized, digestible history-as-entertainment' (Foster 2001: 33). Foster considers these forms of representing the past to be a response to 'hard-nosed motivations in the (supposedly) real world of politics as well as marketing' (Foster 2001: 24). In this environment, beset by commercialism, nostalgia and difference, sustaining the liberal preference for the 'progressivist subject' of the *Up in Arms* exhibition may be increasingly difficult and offers a clue to the collapse of the moderate centre in local politics.

Conclusion

Karl Marx wrote that in a time of revolution or in the creation of something new, spirits of the past are conjured up to serve in the 'new scene of world history' in time-honoured guise. According to Marx, Roman ghosts provided the French bourgeoisie of the nineteenth century the 'self-deceptions that they needed to conceal from themselves the bourgeois limitations of the content of their struggles and to keep their enthusiasm on the high plane of great historical tragedy' (Marx [1852] 2000: 330). In Northern Ireland during 1998 it was the ghosts of the United Irishmen who watched over the cradle of the new 'agreed Ireland' and gave weight to the political ambitions of a relatively weak and fragile liberal constituency. This constituency was made up of moderates within unionism and nationalism; centrists like the cross-community Alliance Party; the Northern Ireland Women's Coalition urging consensus; and organisations like CRC and New Agenda, whose aim it was to 'promote dialogue and public debate' among the local business community, the trade unions, education, the voluntary and community sector and the churches (New Agenda advertisement 1998: 40)[12]. Here was the political centre ground, largely bourgeois in complexion but never amounting to a bourgeoisie.

Its limitations quickly became apparent, not only in the slothful and halting progress made in the political process but ultimately in the loss of executive power to the 'extremes' of the

Democratic Unionist Party and Sinn Féin, which initially seemed to make the achievement of a working political settlement more difficult. This political failure is underscored by the problems liberals have faced constructing a public history. Their self-validating historical narrative of Ireland's tragic past, evident in *Up in Arms*, has given way to the personal reflections of 'ordinary people' in *Conflict: the Irish at War*. It would seem that despite 'the hand of history' visiting Northern Ireland in the run up to the Agreement, public history has been required to disappear along with its progressivist subject; in its place is a subjective look at the past under the guise of 'ordinary people'. In the following two chapters we shall see that this personalising of history and politics is also to be found in film and television drama, where images of domesticated paramilitaries and thoroughly privatised versions of citizenship prevail.

Notes

1. For example, in February 2008 Sinn Féin's proposal to hold a commemoration at Stormont in memory of Mairead Farrell, one of three IRA members shot dead by the SAS in Gibraltar 20 years previously, provoked unionist anger and a counter-proposal to celebrate the achievements of the SAS.
2. BBC (2006), 'Timeline: Northern Ireland's road to peace', http://news.bbc.co.uk/1/hi/northern_ireland/4072261.stm. Accessed 12 November 2009.
3. Downing Street (1993), Joint Declaration, 15 December, p. 3.
4. Community Relations Council (1999), 'What is the Community Relations Council?', http://www.community-relations.org.uk/community relations/overview). Accessed 1999.
5. 'The fact was that retaining control of Ireland was always more important to the British than liberating it was to the French. To encourage their followers to think otherwise, and to gloss over the likely consequences of a successful French invasion, was at best naive of the leaders of the United Irishmen.' Ulster Museum, *Up in Arms exhibition catalogue* 1998: 1.
6. 'By 1798, the leaders of the United Irishmen were no longer united. The question of whether or not to wait for another French expedition to arrive … split the ruling body of the movement. Meanwhile the rank and file became impatient […] With no overall leadership […] the United Irishmen in and around Dublin quickly faded and early successes achieved by surprise in Kildare were soon reversed.' Ulster Museum, *Up in Arms exhibition catalogue* 1998: 197.
7. 'In March 1797 General Lake began the disarmament of Ulster […] The harsh methods used, predictable if the policy was to succeed in its aim, inevitably outraged the people who had to endure them […]' Ulster Museum, *Up in Arms exhibition catalogue* 1998: 155.
8. 'The Irish Parliament had to be persuaded to agree to abolish itself. Being a thoroughly corrupt body, it did so when sufficiently rewarded.' Ulster Museum, *Up in Arms exhibition catalogue* 1998: 271.
9. 'Despite the United Irishmen's campaign for 'a cordial union' in Ireland, sectarian tensions were never far below the surface in late eighteenth century Ireland.' Ulster Museum, *Up in Arms exhibition catalogue* 1998: 10.
10. *Saoirse*, July 1998.
11. *The Irish Times*, 7 June 1999.
12. New Agenda advertisement (1998), *Fortnight*, 369, March/April, p. 40.

Chapter 4

The Changing Image of the Paramilitaries

Two years after the signing of the Good Friday Agreement, David Trimble, then leader of the Ulster Unionist Party, remarked that republicans would need to be 'housetrained' before they could enter the Northern Ireland executive[1]. While the jibe offended Sinn Féin, in reality a process of domesticating the paramilitaries in public perception had already been initiated some time before by the British government. In 1994, during the initial phase of the peace process, they gave Sinn Féin some interesting public relations advice in a secret communiqué, specifically that the party should publicly challenge the British government to sit down to talks. In fact, it was suggested that Sinn Féin should use the analogy of marriage and say, 'We are standing at the altar, why won't (the British) come and join us?' Just days later, Martin McGuinness made the proposal in an interview with *The Guardian* (McLaughlin and Miller 1996: 130). In the same period, the government commissioned a new series of public films for its confidential telephone service. These films portrayed paramilitary figures as ordinary family men with a choice to make between war and peace. This marked a shift in government propaganda that, up until then, had portrayed the paramilitaries, especially republicans, as psychopathic monsters, outside of society and with nothing to offer but 'murder and mayhem'.

This chapter looks at how a range of visual media handled shifting perceptions of the conflict in the North, from war to peace, particularly those of the various paramilitary organisations seen as part of the problem but not necessarily the solution. Yet bringing them in from the cold and involving them in the peace process became a key plank in official government strategy. Throughout the conflict, official propaganda excoriated them. Now, it would have to shift public perception of them to an extent that would make their involvement in politics at least palatable if not desirable for most people.

First, however, it is important to take a brief look at how things used to be, specifically the nature of anti-terrorist propaganda and censorship, if we are fully to understand the true extent of this paradigm shift and the challenges it presented to the media in Britain and Ireland.[2]

Historical context

In many ways, the more relaxed representation of the paramilitaries during the peace process seems extraordinary in the historical context of the conflict in Northern Ireland. In the 1970s and 1980s, British government policy sought to criminalise paramilitary violence and empty it of political content. Censorship and propaganda were key functions of this policy and had a deadening impact on how the media were able to report the conflict. The 1980s, in particular, saw public service broadcasting come into direct confrontation with the government over a number of current affairs programmes and documentaries that appeared to be insufficiently critical of, or even sympathetic to, terrorists.[3] Notable examples here include a programme in the BBC's documentary series *Real Lives*, 'At the Edge of the Union' (BBC 1985) and 'Death on the Rock' (Thames Television 1988), a *This Week* investigation into the shooting of an IRA unit in Gibraltar in 1988.[4]

'At the Edge of the Union' was set in Derry, Northern Ireland's second city, and looked at the lives of two men on opposite sides of the conflict: Martin McGuinness of Sinn Féin and Gregory Campbell, a loyalist politician and member of Ian Paisley's Democratic Unionist Party. The programme provoked controversy ostensibly because it gave voice to Martin McGuinness, whom many suspected was a prominent IRA leader. More precisely, in the words of the programme producer, Paul Hamann, it showed McGuinness with 'a human face',[5] living life in a domestic setting with his wife and children.

The British government initially opposed the broadcast of the film and prompted the BBC Board of Governors to review its contents. This brought the governors into direct conflict with the BBC's director general, Alasdair Milne, who saw the government's interference as a direct threat to the Corporation's independence. Some of governors objected to the programme's 'domestication of the IRA' and their portrayal as 'loveable people with babies' (O'Carroll 2005) and only relented when the producers agreed to re-cut it to include images of IRA violence. Controversies such as these highlight how difficult it was at this time for media producers to work outside of the prevailing and very restrictive, anti-terrorist propaganda framework: depicting the paramilitary with a 'human face' or as a 'family man' was strongly discouraged.[6]

The most famous and controversial conflict between the commercial Independent Television network (ITV) and the government over Northern Ireland involved Thames Television and its *This Week* programme, 'Death on the Rock', which set out to investigate the circumstances surrounding the shooting by British undercover soldiers of three members of the IRA in Gibraltar in 1988. The producers came under fire from the British government and the right-wing press even before the programme was completed and, when it was scheduled to go out, the then Foreign Secretary, Sir Geoffrey Howe, pressurised the Independent Broadcasting Authority (IBA) to withhold it. The IBA resisted and allowed the programme to be broadcast as scheduled. Even the government-appointed Windlesham and Rampton (1989) inquiry cleared the producers of any professional misconduct. BBC Northern Ireland aired its own investigation into events at Gibraltar as part of its current affairs series, *Spotlight*. It was broadcast around the same period as 'Death on the Rock' but was less politically significant in Britain even though it attracted an equal measure of condemnation from certain sections of the local media and public opinion.

Broadcasting in and from Northern Ireland was made even more difficult from October 1988 with the introduction of the 'broadcast ban', a set of restrictions for reporting paramilitary organisations or their political affiliates and sympathisers. The ban applied to all British broadcasters and only to material broadcast within the UK. It required editors and producers to replace with subtitles or an actor's voice the directly spoken words of people such as Sinn Féin president, Gerry Adams, when they appeared as official spokespersons for their organisation. Crucially, the broadcast ban placed the onus of responsibility on producers to decide what was official and what was not, a dilemma that made the production process so cumbersome that they fell back on the default position of excluding direct interviews as much as possible. It was widely accepted that the restrictions were aimed directly at the IRA and Sinn Féin; indeed, research showed a dramatic decline in interviews with Sinn Féin representatives over a one-year period, 1988–89 (Henderson, Reilly and Miller 1990), during which time, unknown to most people, the British government was engaging in secret talks with the IRA about ways to end their military campaign.

Although the ban remained in force until the first IRA ceasefire in 1994, the developing peace process demanded a much more immediate shift in official propaganda, away from an anti-terrorist discourse and towards the possibility that paramilitaries could be brought to the negotiating table. The first clue of a change of tone came at the outset of the peace process, not from the media but crucially from the British government in the form of TV advertisements for its confidential anti-terrorist telephone service.

Selling the Peace? The confidential telephone advertisements

The confidential telephone service was set up by the Northern Ireland Office (NIO) in the 1970s to receive anonymous information from the public regarding paramilitary activity. It was publicised through a variety of media but of most interest here are the television advertisement campaigns. The early campaigns were strictly anti-terrorist in orientation and fitted into the wider British propaganda framework. Terrorism had no political content or context and the terrorists themselves were portrayed as ruthless, psychotic criminals. For example, *A Future* (NIO 1988) features a young man reflecting on the future for his wife and child in a community dominated by paramilitary violence. What, he asks on his odyssey around his troubled city, have these 'hard men' ever done for him? 'They've left me with no job and no hope, they've wrecked where I live, they've hijacked our cars, they've fed off our backs, and when I saw their kind of justice, I thought there's gotta be something better than this.' This voiceover accompanies images of a war-torn urban environment: bombs exploding, punishment shootings in back alleys and paramilitaries collecting funds in local pubs. The lighting is dark and the atmosphere foreboding, an effect heightened by a crime thriller score.

The NIO continued the service into the 1990s and the period of the peace process but the new circumstances brought a perceptible shift in emphasis in the advertisement campaigns. One only has to note the dramatic visual contrast between the despair of *A Future* and the biblical message of hope in *A New Era*, from 1994, in which the traditional symbols of conflict and division are transformed before our eyes into images of peace and prosperity. A paramilitary gun morphs into a starting pistol for the Belfast marathon; security bollards turn into flower displays; a police cordon turns into ceremonial tape for the opening of a new motorway; and two Royal Ulster Constabulary (RUC) constables reunite a lost child with his mother, confounding the controversial history and nature of the force.[7]

However, we want to focus here on two adverts from 1993 – *Lady* and *I Wanna Be Like You*. This is because they broke most radically from the traditional formal conventions of the confidential telephone adverts shown up until then and since. Far from the usual montage of propaganda images and messages, these ads were constructed as mini-domestic dramas that represented the paramilitary with a more human face, thus situating him in a more ambiguous position in society.

Lady tells the story of two women whose lives are blighted by violence. The ethno-religious identity of the women is not made explicit: they are both portrayed as victims. One is a widow whose husband is murdered by a paramilitary. The other is married to the paramilitary who is imprisoned for the murder. A female narrator intones, 'Two women, two traditions, two tragedies. One married to the victim of violence, one married to the prisoner of violence. Both scarred, both suffering, both desperately wanting it to stop.' As with *A Future*, *Lady* is about the impact of violence on domestic relations except, in this instance, violence is presented as equally tragic for the paramilitaries as it is for their victims.

I Wanna Be Like You also reflects upon the cost of paramilitary violence to family relations, specifically those of father and son. There is no voiceover narrative to this film. Instead it is accompanied by a version of the Harry Chapin song, 'Cat in the Cradle'. It presents a man's journey over a number of years from paramilitarism to his recognition of the futility of violence. In the beginning, he neglects his family, ends up in prison and eventually sees his son grow up and follow in his footsteps as a paramilitary. The son in turn becomes remote from the father and is shown gunning down a man in front of his child, emphasising the cyclical nature of the violence. The son eventually loses his life to violence and the advert closes with the image of his father grieving at his grave.

After the paramilitary ceasefires in 1994, the NIO commissioned a very different series of public films that moved away from the anti-terrorist message altogether. Broadcast during the summer of 1995, these made no mention of the confidential phone service or of terrorists or terrorism. Indeed, they appeared to have no specific purpose except to show off Northern Ireland as a place where people enjoyed life without fear of violence. Scored with some of the best-known songs of Van Morrison, a native of Belfast, such as 'Brown Eyed Girl', 'Days Like This', and 'Have I Told You Lately', the four films have the glossy look of tourist advertisements, marketing peace in Northern Ireland as consumer commodity. In the first film, *Northern Irish Difference*, babies and toddlers play at a crèche, oblivious to sectarian or cultural difference; in the second, *Northern Irish Life*, two boys from both traditions play on a beach and innocently exchange what would, in the conflict of the past, have been seen as sectarian badges of identity – King Billy for Glasgow Celtic Football Club! The third film, *Northern Irish Quality*, celebrates the sporting and cultural achievements of people like

Mary Peters, George Best and Liam Neeson, while the fourth, *Northern Irish Spirit*, reminds people of the region's stunning coastal and rural scenery. All the films in the series end with Van Morrison's epithet from 'Coney Island', 'Wouldn't it be great if it was like this all the time?' and the on-screen slogan, 'Time for the Bright Side'. The use of Morrison's music in this series of films came with his explicit permission and blessing and reveals much about the heady, optimistic mood that gripped Northern Ireland in the hot summer of 1995.

When the IRA ceasefire ended in 1996, with bombs in London and Manchester, the NIO returned to the violent imagery of the early confidential telephone advertisements. However, the restoration of the ceasefires and the negotiations towards the Good Friday Agreement in 1998 brought a return to optimism. During the referendum campaign in May that year, the NIO distributed to every home a copy of the Agreement document, its cover showing the archetypal nuclear family silhouetted against a rising sun, symbolising the Agreement as a new dawn for the people of Northern Ireland. It was revealed later that the picture was actually of a sunset and was taken in South Africa, perfect dawns being difficult to catch in Northern Ireland. Still, these idealised, post-ceasefire images marked a radical departure from the violent imagery of 1988 and *A Future*, and even from the more positive advertisements of the early 1990s because they dispensed with the anti-terrorist message altogether and held out the prospect of real peace and a final settlement to the conflict.

Martin McLoone (1993, 1996, 1997) was one of the first media academics to take a serious look at these government films and spot the subtle change of message in their narrative and photography. As he has argued, they did indeed appear to prepare the public for negotiations with the enemy while at the same time suggest to the IRA especially that they had something to gain by laying down their arms. However, the films may also have had the effect of giving the media licence to explore the ongoing transition from war to peace in ways unthinkable just years before. One of these was to interview former paramilitaries about their role in the conflict, to show us the gunmen with a human face without provoking the kind of political backlash that blighted the *Real Lives* programme.

Talking to the enemy

The lifting of broadcasting censorship in Britain and Ireland in 1994 was widely seen as part of the deal to bring about the IRA ceasefire in August that year but it took some time for television producers to come to terms with the more relaxed regime. They still demonstrated a knee-jerk reflex to confront and cajole republican and loyalist figures about their history of violence rather than try to understand their motivations.

A good example of this was an edition in late 1994 of *The Late, Late Show* (RTÉ 1994), Irish television's longest running chat show (modelled on America's *Tonight* show with Johnny Carson), which had as a guest, Gerry Adams, president of Sinn Féin. There were two unique and controversial aspects about his appearance that had more to do with the legacy of Ireland's previous censorship regime and thus an overly cautious editorial policy than with Adams himself. First, the presenter, Gay Byrne, declined to greet him with a handshake, as he usually did with all his guests, and described him in a deeply uneasy introduction as 'the most controversial man in Ireland'. Second, after a short interview, Byrne proceeded to moderate a confrontation between Adams and four hostile panellists. The encounter was tense and heated but Adams was widely perceived by the live audience and by television critics to have handled it calmly and expertly. Indeed, in the following days, RTÉ received a record number of viewer complaints that the treatment of Adams was unbalanced and unfair. The following year, *The Late, Late Show* invited Adams back for an exclusively one-to-one interview with Byrne in which he discussed his background and politics, his thoughts about the peace process and his private interests.

Like the political process itself, television was taking time to change and adapt to the new circumstances that peace afforded. But change it did and in the late 1990s the BBC broadcast three major series that examined the conflict from the perspective of the principal protagonists: *Provos* (1997), *Loyalists* (1999) and *Brits* (2000). Public reaction to them was muted, although critics expressed concern about the BBC's timing of *Provos*, believing that it might in some way undermine the peace process in a crucial and delicate phase – the beginning of formal multi-party talks on 15 September 1997 – and that the producers were giving airtime to active members of the IRA. Executive producer, Steve Hewlett, claimed that the producers:

> [did not] seek interviews with people currently active in the IRA but it is not an open organisation; people do not wear badges and there is a distinct possibility that some were not telling the truth. But if we knew they were active, we wouldn't use them. (*The Times*, 6 August 1997)

The programmes in the *Provos* and *Loyalists* series are structured around interviews mainly with ex-paramilitaries but there are also contributions from their victims and from politicians and public figures who were prominent in the 1960s and 1970s when the violence was at its most sustained. These are intercut with a narrative history of political violence and punctuated with some remarkable and hitherto unseen archive film footage of key moments in the history of the conflict. However, in other respects, both series are ultimately safe and uncontroversial. They merely confirm prejudice and assumptions rather than challenge them. They are case studies in murder, narratives about ruthless IRA bombers and loyalist death squads. Conducted in stark light against a black background, they are at once interrogative and voyeuristic.

The series *Loyalists*, in particular, features some brutally frank, matter-of-fact admissions of murder from ex-paramilitaries. Jim Light, a former member of the Ulster Freedom Fighters, tells the presenter, Peter Taylor, how he led the abduction and murder of a young Catholic man in retaliation for the murder by the IRA of six Protestant pensioners. It must be said here that the rendering of this interview in print lacks the impact of viewing this doleful, deadbeat exchange between Taylor and Light:

Taylor: What did you do?
Light: I went out with a group of other volunteers from the UFF [Ulster Freedom Fighters] and we picked up a Catholic and we took him away and we executed him.
Taylor: Murdered him?
Light: Yeah.
Taylor: Shot him dead?
Light: Yes.
Taylor: A Catholic?
Light: Yes.
Taylor: Any Catholic?
Light: Yes.
Taylor: Why was he selected?
Light: He was selected for no other reason than he was a Catholic.
Taylor: No reason to believe he was involved in the republican movement?
Light: No.
Taylor: Just an innocent, 17 year old student?
Light: Yeah.
Taylor: Who pulled the trigger?
Light: I pulled the trigger.
Taylor: You pulled the trigger?
Light: I did, yes.
Taylor: Without any hesitation?
Light: [Pause] No, actually, no. I wouldn't say I had any hesitation at that time.

Of course, this style of interview is quite common in television's 'true crime' genre. It may reveal much about the psychological state of the killer but little of the political impulses behind his action. The focus is on 'coming clean': close-ups invite the viewer to judge the demeanour of the interviewee and render a verdict on their honesty and the plausibility of their remorse. Then, as if to prejudice the verdict, each interview closes with a prison photograph and details of conviction and sentence: 'Jim Light was sentenced to life for murder'.

Yet there are entry points for further inquiry here that are tantalisingly followed up only for the trail to go cold. Bobby Morton, once a loyalist paramilitary, tells Taylor that some prominent unionist politicians of the day, such as the Reverend Ian Paisley, had much to answer for in stirring up loyalist violence:

Morton: They were only too happy to lead us by the nose at one stage – 'Get into them boys! Protestant Ulster! We will fight and we will die!' Well, *they* never fought and *they* never died. It was left to people like me.

Taylor then takes this point up with Paisley, who admits that paramilitaries like Morton were among the ranks of his supporters in those days but insists that he could not be held responsible for their crimes which, he says, he condemned outright and duly disowned at that time.

In this important respect, therefore, the *Provos* and *Loyalists* series failed to look at the politics and ideology that motivated and sustained the paramilitaries and see their politics in some instances fixed and unbending but, in others, fluid and flexible. Nonetheless, they marked a new permissiveness in current affairs broadcasting, taking advantage of the end of censorship to give voice and a human face to people who, until recently, issued terse statements to the media behind balaclava masks.

Remembering the past for the needs of the present

The need for accountability and remorse for violence during the conflict is one of the most difficult and, so far, unresolved issues of the peace process in Northern Ireland; there is yet no agreement about how to bring about constructive encounters between perpetrators and victims of violence. However, in 2006, the BBC tried with *Facing the Truth* (BBC 2006), a series of three programmes aired over successive nights and moderated by a panel of three experts including Bishop Desmond Tutu. The programmes featured encounters between loyalist and republican paramilitaries, and also British soldiers, and the victims of their past violence, whether survivors or bereaved relatives, and encouraged the participants to work towards some kind of reckoning or reconciliation.

For critics such as Bill Rolston, the series was 'a bold and imaginative step' on the part of the BBC but was not without its problems (Rolston 2007: 335). Firstly, the format and the type of encounters it generated bordered on 'reality television', a potentially exploitative and voyeuristic form of entertainment. For example, an encounter between loyalist paramilitary, Michael Stone, and the widow and brother of one of his victims, Dermot Hackett, took up the entire third programme and made for uncomfortable and dramatic viewing. But there is evidence of a significant degree of editorial manipulation to create the drama at the expense of very vulnerable participants. Secondly, although billed as an opportunity for victims to tell their story, to be heard and remembered, there was no doubt that editorial control remained firmly with the broadcaster, in this case the BBC, whose role during the conflict was hardly neutral.[8] Thirdly, the programme's definition of victim does not allow for the possibility that the perpetrators of violence might themselves be victims of the conflict and the extreme circumstances that brought it about. And fourthly, Rolston argues, the religious overtones to the experiment, underlined by Bishop Tutu's persistent references to God and God's forgiveness: 'allowed no space for those with more secular definitions [and] became in effect a denial of a political approach to dealing with the past that looked beyond interpersonal encounters to the structural causes of conflict and violence' (Rolston 2007: 359).

Rolston's remarks on the production decisions behind the *Facing the Truth* series are not isolated. They should be considered in the context of public unease about the degree of manipulation involved, the shoehorning of very specific, individual stories into a predetermined framework of liberal assumptions about what is required from a process of reconciliation and even restorative justice for the bereaved and hurt of the conflict to find some kind of closure.

The BBC film, *Five Minutes of Heaven* (Hirschbiegel 2009), centres on the making of a programme very much in the mould of *Facing the Truth*. Although the drama is ultimately serious in its intent, it takes a satirical poke at the fictional television company and its preoccupation to get the right shot, the ideal sound quality and the maximum degree of dramatic tension as it constructs a confrontation between one-time loyalist paramilitary, Alistair Little, and a Catholic victim of his past violence, Joe Griffin, whose brother he murdered. Indeed, *Five Minutes of Heaven* rejects the liberal intent behind truth and reconciliation processes and instead suggests two, much more controversial possibilities. The first, and this resonates with Bill Rolston's objections to *Facing the Truth*, is that the perpetrator might be as much a prisoner of his past as the victim. Alistair Little is depicted as an isolated individual who, when not giving testimony on truth and reconciliation junkets around the world, lives alone in a sparsely furnished flat in Belfast. A production assistant describes him to Joe Griffin as 'a broken man'. The second is that closure for the victim can only really come through some form of violent catharsis, the 'five minutes of heaven' suggested in the drama's title. Unable finally to face Little, Joe Griffin backs out of the production but Little conspires to contact him privately and arrange a meeting in a derelict house, once the Griffin home where the murder took place. The two men wrestle in an upstairs room until they eventually fall out of the window onto the street below. The writer of the drama, Guy Hibbert, explains that he:

> first started out thinking this would be about truth and reconciliation and all those rather clichéd thoughts. I had a quite a simplistic view, I suppose [but] I learned through the process that it's a lot more complicated than those awful simplistic words like 'closure' and 'forgiveness'. It's incredibly tough. (*The Independent*, 3 April 2009)

There are very few examples of less adversarial, more enlightened television about the causes of the conflict and its aftermath. One of the most interesting is *Somme Journey* (BBC Northern Ireland 2002), a short documentary produced by BBC Northern Ireland and first broadcast in 2002. The programme brought together former enemies, Tom Hartley of Sinn Féin and the late David Ervine, leader of the Progressive Unionist Party and once prominent member of the loyalist paramilitary Ulster Volunteer Force, for a visit to the First World War graves of the Somme, in France. The encounter was not only politically unprecedented for television but also provided both men, and therefore the viewer, with new insights into how loyalist and republican versions of history have been couched more in myth than in fact.

Commemoration of the war dead has always been central to the identity and cultural expression of the wider Ulster unionist family but traditionally taboo for the Irish republican movement. So while unionists would commemorate annually the mainly Protestant men of the Ulster divisions and those serving in other British regiments, republicans and, indeed, the nationalist establishment North and South of Ireland, denied totally the sacrifice of young Irish nationalists who joined other regiments of the British Army and fell alongside their Protestant compatriots. At the same time, and until very recently, the unionist history and mythology of Ulster's sacrifice rarely made reference to that of Irish nationalists. For Ervine and Hartley to acknowledge all this on camera, in a spirit of grace and generosity and without compromising their core values, marked a genuinely unique moment on television and underpinned efforts North and South to promote more inclusive models of commemoration of this key event in unionist and nationalist history. But the programme also showed that it is possible for television to move away from the adversarial model so typical of current affairs coverage of the conflict; and it illustrated the potential for the medium to promote insight through dialogue rather than entrenchment through confrontation. As David Ervine put it on *Somme Journey*, it offered nationalists and unionists the opportunity to 'switch on the light' and 'explore' the past.

While factual television had to work within clearly defined, institutional structures to explore the conflict and the peace, fictional film and television drama could avail of relatively more open visual and narrative forms. The following sections look at how they represented paramilitaries and their struggle to negotiate the changing political circumstances of the peace process.

Film and television drama

The dramatic contrast in imagery between 'strife-torn maelstrom' and 'blissful, rural idyll', typifies two of the most prevalent, visual representations of Ireland in the 20th Century and, as John Hill (1987) has shown, it is the former image that has dominated cinematic portrayals of the North. The Carol Reed film, *Odd Man Out* (Reed 1947), is an antecedent of this tradition. The film follows Johnny McQueen, a leader of the 'organisation' (a euphemism for the IRA), who is wounded in an armed robbery and escapes into the city before he and his sweetheart, Kathleen, are shot by the police, their romantic intentions unfulfilled. While Hill acknowledges the film's very distinctive visual style, he argues that its narrative is typical of cinematic representations of the Irish conflict, in that it ignores political and historical context, reducing violence to 'a manifestation of the Irish "national" character' (Hill 1987: 149) and maintaining rigid ideological closure.

However, what has been termed 'ceasefire cinema' appears to offer films with at least some moral and political ambiguity in their representation of the paramilitary, if not the violence he deploys. This is much in the same way as we have seen in the NIO's confidential telephone adverts, *Lady* and *Wanna Be Like You*, but without, perhaps, such overtly propagandistic images and messages. Much of the ambiguity arises out of a mixture of genres and generic conventions that make a straightforward propaganda analysis impossible. Instead, we can draw a much clearer distinction based on a relation between genre and subject matter: in other words, a mix of crime thriller and horror among those films that feature loyalist paramilitaries; and political thriller and melodrama among those concerned mainly with republicans.

Of course, this has ideological consequences for how the subject matter is dealt with. Film portrayals of loyalist paramilitaries as underworld criminals (*Nothing Personal* – O'Sullivan 1996) or psychopathic monsters (*Resurrection Man* – Evans 1998) reinforce dominant caricatures of loyalists as being driven or sometimes even trapped by venal motivations and constraints rather than informed by a political ideology or manifesto. By contrast, a mix of the political thriller/melodrama in films such as *Love Lies Bleeding* (Winterbottom 1993) and *The Boxer* (Sheridan 1997) accommodates the republican subject as a man in control of his destiny, the narrative driving him in a direction away from violence towards a peaceful settlement, whether in the political or domestic sphere. In a sense, such contradistinctive, generic portrayals reflect the mood of the period, the 1990s, with loyalism low in political confidence and wracked by violent internal feuds and dissent, all in stark contrast to their more politically confident and united republican counterparts.

Loyalists

Until recently, loyalists and northern Protestants were generally absent or marginal in cinematic representations of Ireland and the conflict (McIlroy 1998; Baker 2001). Protestants were more visible in television drama productions such as the BBC's trilogy of plays about a young Protestant, Billy Martin: *Too Late to Talk to Billy* (1982), *A Matter of Choice for Billy* (1983) and *A Coming to Terms for Billy* (1984). However, these plays were dramatisations of working-class family life rather than loyalism.

It was only after the ceasefires that loyalists finally made it to the centre of the big screen in *Nothing Personal* and *Resurrection Man* where they are portrayed in a thoroughly abject light (Baker 2001 and 2004). This abjection manifested itself in the failure of their loyalist protagonists to achieve and maintain domesticated heterosexuality and their association with dysfunctional sexualities that account for their violent proclivities. In *Resurrection Man*, loyalist gang leader Victor Kelly is in the grip of an Oedipal crisis – too enamoured of his indulgent mother and seemingly disinterested in consummating his relationship with his promiscuous girlfriend, Heather. Victor's libido seems only to be sated by the blood of his victims, whom he murders in particularly brutal ways. If that was not enough to signify his social and psychological dysfunction, the film also alludes to his homosexuality and possible paedophilia. In a particularly heavy-handed scene, he is shown drinking and taking drugs with a senior loyalist, McClure. The two get intimate and, as McClure fingers the features of Victor's face, Victor asks to see again a set of photographs depicting 'English boys in bed together' (Baker 2004: 78–86).

In the film *Nothing Personal*, homosexuality also lies beneath the surface of the homosocial world of gang membership, and in particular the relationship between Kenny, the loyalist gang leader, and his right hand man, Ginger. Initiation into the gang takes the form of a perverse marriage ceremony with its oaths of loyalty and fidelity. The sexual tensions underlying this process and gang membership generally are emphasised by the violent and apparently jealous reaction of Ginger to the initiation of a new recruit. And as if to offset anxieties about this underlying homosexuality, the gang frequently indulges in graphic, misogynist banter and jokes about the sexual preferences of rivals.

Kenny's estrangement from heterosexual domesticity is apparent in his separation from his wife, typically on account of his violent convictions, although the film does hold out the possibility of romantic redemption in the chance encounter between Kenny's wife, Anne, and Liam, a single, Catholic father. On a night of rioting, Liam leaves his children to defend his home and district from encroaching loyalist rioters but gets stranded on the wrong side of the peace line and is beaten up. Anne finds him on the street and brings him into her home to recover, where there is clearly a growing intimacy between the couple. But, when Liam resumes his journey home, he is abducted by Kenny and his gang. They take him to a loyalist drinking den and proceed to torture him until Kenny suddenly recognises his victim as a childhood friend. He orders an end to the torture and sees Liam home safely. When, later in the film, Ginger threatens to shoot Liam, Kenny wounds his comrade in the leg. Events take a tragic turn when a Catholic youth tries to exact revenge on the loyalist gang, but accidentally kills Liam's daughter. Sorry for Liam's loss and revolted by Ginger's pleasure at the girl's death, Kenny shoots Ginger.

Again there are similarities here between *Nothing Personal* and *Resurrection Man*, in that both films suggest that their loyalist protagonists are assassinated at the behest of their superiors. In *Resurrection Man*, McClure has Victor Kelly assassinated when his violence escalates beyond control. In *Nothing Personal*, loyalist leader, Leonard Wilson, orders Kenny to shoot his friend Ginger, whose violent behaviour begins to threaten a recently brokered ceasefire between loyalists and republicans. Kenny vacillates at first but resolves to follow orders when he is finally confronted with the depths of Ginger's depravity. His hesitation, however, proves fatal when Wilson sets him and his gang up for an ambush by the British Army.

As the Beast Sleeps (Bradbeer 2002) is a significantly different sort of depiction of loyalism from those in *Nothing Personal* and *Resurrection Man*. A single TV drama based on a stage play by Gary Mitchell, it employs a degree of realism in its bleak but sometimes empathetic portrayal of a local Ulster Defence Association (UDA) 'team' in Belfast, marginalised by a peace process that offers little to them in the way of hope or prospects for a better life in the 'new Northern Ireland'. In fact, the politics of the peace process, adopted and promoted by the UDA's political leadership, threaten to shatter the bonds that hold the unit together under its leader, Kyle. Whereas *Resurrection Man* and *Nothing Personal* draw on the aesthetics of the horror and gangster genres, reducing loyalist violence and motivation to a psychopathology, *As the Beast Sleeps* deploys a set of social realist conventions that emphasises the social environment within which its characters exist and which restricts their options.

The drama is structured around the relationship between Kyle, his wife Sandra and his impatient, hot-headed comrade and friend, Freddie. Freddie is godfather to Kyle and

Sandra's son, Joe, and is frequently referred to as 'uncle'. The men's relationship then is often brotherly, but at other times Kyle seems more like a father-figure to his more impetuous, childish friend. Freddie's inclusion in Kyle's family and his membership of the UDA 'team' erodes the distinction between political and domestic spheres that is such a feature of many other films in this period.

The film opens against the political backdrop of the ceasefire announced by loyalist paramilitary groups in 1994, a development that not only marginalises Kyle, Freddie and the rest of the 'foot-soldiers', but also puts a strain on Kyle's family, which eventually comes apart when Sandra leaves him. She is opposed to the peace process and concerned at the family's loss of income, so when Freddie robs the local loyalist bar she is a willing accomplice, hiding the stolen money for him. Her actions compromise Kyle's position in the UDA and at the end he is left an isolated figure with neither comrades nor family. It is the fear of exclusion, then, that lies at the heart of *As the Beast Sleeps*.

When the loyalist leadership orders all units to stand down and desist from paramilitary or criminal activity in the interests of political progress, Kyle obeys but sees the peace process as a temporary distraction from his team's work of illegal fundraising. However, the political leadership sees things rather differently. In a key scene, loyalist paramilitary leader-cum-politician, Alec, orders battalion commander, Larry, to enforce political as well as military discipline among foot soldiers such as Kyle and his comrades, telling him that:

these violent young men have no place [...] in our future. [...] God forgive us, we were violent young men once, right or wrong, but we've changed and now everyone else has to change. And afterwards [...] there will be a place for you, a better place.

The film then sets up an opposition between those determined to secure their position in that 'better place' and those who will be left behind. In this respect, Kyle, his comrades and his family are in a precarious position, indicated by their antagonistic relationship with the local loyalist bar that they once supplied with cigarettes and alcohol. The bar has become a legitimate business and has no more need of Kyle and Freddie's contraband, leaving them effectively unemployed. As a scene in the Job Centre makes clear, their lack of formal qualifications renders them suitable for only the most menial of jobs. Insult is added to injury when Jack, the bar's obsequious and enterprising manager, makes clear that their very presence in the bar is a liability: 'Every time these fucking Comanches come in here it pegs us back. People are feeling uncomfortable and intimidated. That's not the atmosphere that I want to create here and it's not an atmosphere that's good for business'.

Jack is Kyle and Freddie's ever-present antagonist, more so than republicans, who are referred to in hostile terms throughout the drama but who never actually appear. It is Jack who poses the most immediate and obvious threat to Kyle and Freddie. As manager of the loyalist bar, he effectively replaces the 'team' as the revenue stream that funds the political ambitions of the loyalist leadership. There is seemingly no place in the new dispensation for grassroots loyalists like Kyle and Freddie now that they are an economic liability and surplus to political requirement. That exclusion is both acute and symbolic in Freddie's case when he is banned from the loyalist bar, which he then robs in frustration and anger. Consequently the UDA leadership orders Kyle to find him, punish him and reclaim the money, an order he carries out, leaving him estranged from his friend and his wife, who it transpires has hidden the money for Freddie. She leaves Kyle in disgust despite his protestations that he had no choice but to act as he did, which echoes an earlier attempt by Kyle to explain to Freddie their predicament: 'this is the way things are going to go no matter what we do'. *As the Beast Sleeps*' social realist conventions mean that the political and social contexts presented in the film do more to determine the drama than the psychological dispositions of characters like Kyle. However, his apparent loss of agency and his conviction that 'this is the way things are going' no matter what he and his comrades do, seems to comment on the 'no alternative' discourse that has attended the political process in Northern Ireland and that we looked at in chapter 2.

Republicans

The dark dystopia of loyalism in *Nothing Personal* and *Resurrection Man*, or even the sense of powerlessness and betrayal in *As the Beast Sleeps*, stands in sharp contrast to the seemingly positive depictions of republicans in films such as *Love Lies Bleeding* or *The Boxer*. We say 'seemingly' because there is a strong undertow of conservatism in these films that make no concessions to progressivism in either form or content. They take the form of political thrillers or domestic melodramas, in some cases both, and drive their protagonists to a narrative closure of apolitical domestication rather than public engagement with the political process.

The Boxer measures the impact of political violence on domestic and private relations but it goes further to suggest that paramilitaries may have a role in forging rather than destroying such relations. The central character in the film is Danny, a republican ex-prisoner who tries to rekindle his affair with former lover, Maggie. However, she is already married to an IRA man still serving time in prison and Danny's advances towards her provoke consternation in the republican community. Indeed, it makes him a target for Harry, a hardline republican, who considers their relationship a betrayal of the incarcerated husband. Harry rejects the peace process and is further outraged by the fact that Danny has turned away from political violence. The two then are set on a collision course, threatening Danny's relationship with Maggie.

Significantly, their relationship is saved not by the forces of law and order but by the violent intervention of Maggie's father, Joe Hamill, himself a senior republican and architect of the peace strategy. Hamill commissions Harry's murder, simultaneously securing the ceasefire and a successful romantic conclusion to Maggie and Danny's affair. The film closes with a scene in which Danny and Maggie are stopped at an RUC checkpoint. An officer asks them where they are going. 'We're going home,' says Maggie. There are no further questions and the police officer waves them on their way. Even the RUC, ostensibly the malevolent foe of northern nationalism, cannot object to such a natural and plainly righteous destination.

McLoone argues that Joe Hamill stands in a cinematic tradition of IRA men who are in many ways 'more sympathetic and more flexible' than some of their hardline comrades. In this way, *The Boxer* confirms a post-ceasefire politics that presents the way forward as being 'through compromise and accommodation' (McLoone 2000: 78). However, this misses the crucial significance of Harry's assassination. Far from the optimistic conclusion of peace 'through compromise and accommodation', the film alludes to some of the uncomfortable choices that lie ahead for republicans, namely policing dissent within their own ranks – by violent means if necessary.

As with *The Boxer*, *Love Lies Bleeding* ends with the elimination of dissident elements by supporters of the republican peace strategy. However, unlike *The Boxer*, this violent action destroys rather rescues the romantic intentions of its protagonist. Written by Ronan Bennett, the drama explores the ambiguities, contradictions and compromises inherent in bringing a campaign of political violence to an end. Broadcast in September 1993, the drama was conceived prior to the public admission of the British government that they had been talking to republicans and it predates the IRA's ceasefire by almost a year. The story is told from the point of view of Conn, an IRA prisoner on day release who is determined to find out the truth about the death of his lover, Layla. His quest coincides with attempts by IRA chief, Thomas Macken, to initiate a ceasefire, a proposal that is violently opposed by hardliners in the movement. It transpires that Layla was one such hardliner and her assassination was carried out on Macken's orders. Further killings ensue, including the slaying of the IRA faction opposed to the peace strategy at the hands of Macken and his supporters. This action clears the way for the announcement of the ceasefire that is greeted with jubilation by republican inmates back at the prison. Meanwhile, Conn is left to come to terms with the notion that political imperatives have taken precedence over his private life, specifically his relationship with Layla. As Macken explains, 'Death here isn't just a personal thing'.

The Boxer and *Love Lies Bleeding* stand in sharp contrast to earlier cinematic representations of the conflict, such as *Odd Man Out*. In the latter, it is the police, and so by implication the state, that dispatches dissidents such as Johnny McQueen, rather than his superiors in the 'organisation'. As John Hill makes clear, the state in this film is 'not only exempt from political enquiry but, at least implicitly, legitimated as the repository of a divine and absolute justice' (Hill 1987: 160).

However, in many of the films considered here, the state is presented as ambivalent, pernicious or lacking. In *Nothing Personal* it arrives belatedly in the shape of the British Army to finish off the loyalist gang. In *Resurrection Man* its representative, Herbie Ferguson, a CID man, is conscientious but impotent. In *Love Lies Bleeding*, the state is largely usurped by IRA chief, Thomas Macken, who acts to secure the peace by luring dissidents into a lethal ambush. In *The Boxer*, the state's role is reduced to one of surveillance, represented by searchlights and the noise of overhead helicopters. In its place stands the IRA leader, Joe Hamill, who defends the social order by policing dissent, securing the peace strategy and defending the new domesticated republicanism represented by Danny, Maggie and her son. Seen in this light, Hamill represents a republicanism shorn of its radical potential and pressed into the service of preserving a social order based on political agnosticism and privatised citizenship.

Situation comedy

While some film and television dramas in the period of the peace process represented paramilitary figures in authoritative and increasingly constitutional roles, television also offered images of them as comic grotesques. In 1994, the year following the broadcast of *Love Lies Bleeding*, the BBC aired *The Empire Laughs Back* (BBC 1994) as part of its *25 Bloody Years* season to mark the anniversary of the troubles. This was a one-off special that featured a number of Irish stand-up comedians performing at the Empire Comedy Club in Belfast. Their routines plundered Northern Ireland politics for humour, a risky venture given that a previous attempt at satire on BBC Northern Ireland had met with vocal opposition from local politicians and public figures across the community. On that occasion, *The Show* (BBC Northern Ireland 1989–1991), which consisted of chat, music and comedy sketches that often lampooned Northern Ireland politics, was eventually forced to water down its content and become a conventional variety show.

The Hole in the Wall Gang, an ensemble of local comedians, featured in both *The Show* and *The Empire Laughs Back*. In 1995, the BBC broadcast their satirical comedy, *Two Ceasefires and a Wedding*, which for the first time on television depicted thoroughly domesticated versions of loyalist and republican paramilitary types. *Two Ceasefires and a Wedding* (BBC Northern Ireland 1995) was in effect the pilot for the sitcom series, *Give My Head Peace* (BBC Northern Ireland), which ran from 1996 to 2007. Both marked a departure for television comedy in Northern Ireland. Previous sitcoms set in Belfast, such as *Foreign Bodies* (BBC Northern Ireland 1986–1987) and *So You Think You've Got Troubles* (BBC Northern Ireland 1991), were much more reticent about the representation of political militants.

Give My Head Peace contains its belligerents within the domestic context of an extended family, albeit a comically dysfunctional one. Emer, the daughter of an ardent republican, marries Billy, an RUC officer and the nephew of vociferous loyalist, Uncle Andy. She moves in with Billy, and together they share a house with Uncle Andy, who is outraged at having a Catholic living in his home. His disdain is mirrored by Emer's father, Da, and her brother, Cal, who abhor their loyalist in-laws. The show's attempts at humour derive from the truculent behaviour of its loyalist and republican characters and their potential to disrupt 'normal' family life. In this respect, Emer's mother, known only as Ma, provides a measure of apolitical and simple-minded domestic probity in contrast to the comically portrayed political passions of the men.

In *Give My Head Peace*, the domestic context renders its belligerent characters 'safe', mapping Northern Ireland's unruly politics onto the comfortingly familiar institution of the family. As with all film and television comedy, the spectators' laughter secures them in a position of superiority and power in relation to the text and its characters (Neale and Krutnik 1990: 80). Meanwhile the cyclical nature of the sitcom narrative works to ensure that no matter what comic outrages or upheavals occur in the show each week, relatively normal family life is reinstated by the end of each episode. This means that despite the sectarian rhetoric and antics of Da, Uncle Andy and their respective ensemble of republican and loyalist associates, essential family relations are unaffected.

Conclusion

It is clear that the changing emphasis in the NIO's confidential telephone advertisements signalled a more relaxed approach in official quarters as to how the media should cover the conflict and the developing peace process. That and the lifting of the broadcast ban in 1994 allowed television current affairs the opportunity to respond positively to the new political and cultural dispensation, to move from the restrictive parameters of the anti-terrorist paradigm to a less censorious, more exploratory analysis of the motivations and objectives of the paramilitaries. The extent to which they availed of this opportunity is questionable. While *Provos* and *Loyalists* featured interviews with paramilitaries in a way unthinkable at the height of the conflict, the series still worked within quite restrictive editorial parameters that inhibited rather than promoted explanation and understanding. And while the *Facing the Truth* series attempted to explore the legacy of paramilitary violence, its set-piece encounters between paramilitaries and their victims seemed more voyeuristic and exploitative than truly insightful. Only *Somme Journey* seemed to offer an alternative approach that provides engagement and dialogue rather than confrontation, opening up possibilities for reviewing the past in new ways.

The most insightful dramatic representation of paramilitaries in this period was *As the Beast Sleeps*, which situated its protagonists in a specific social environment that accounted for their restricted choices. Other representations of paramilitaries took the form of either thrillers and/or melodramas or gangster and/or horror films. As a consequence, they owed more to generic convention than social and political circumstance.

Notes

1. *The Guardian*, 29 May 2000.
2. For more detailed analyses of media politics in this period, see Butler 1995; Curtis 1988; and Miller 1994.
3. This should be seen in wider historical context of Thatcherite hostility to the very concept of public service television in general and to news reporting of other controversial events in the 1980s such as the Falklands War in 1981 and the US bombing of Libya in 1986. See McLaughlin 2000.

4. For detailed, academic accounts of the media politics surrounding these controversies, see Miller 1994; and McLaughlin 2000. Also, from a journalist's perspective, Ian Jack (1988) provides an impression of the prevailing professional and political pressures put upon journalists to report the official propaganda version rather than the facts of what really happened on the Rock of Gibraltar in 1988.
5. Interviewed on: BBC2 (1993) 'The Information War', *Late Show*.
6. For professional perspectives on local broadcast news and current affairs coverage of the conflict see Baker 1996; Bolton 1996; Cathcart 1984; Francis 1996; Kyle 1996; and Leapman 1996.
7. Policing in Northern Ireland had always been a difficult issue, especially among republicans and nationalists, whose leaders long suspected the traditionally Protestant force of collusion with loyalist paramilitaries. It has since been reformed as part of the peace process, with new structures of public accountability, a representative recruitment strategy, a community dimension and a new name, The Police Service of Northern Ireland or PSNI. For a critical discussion, see O'Rawe 2008.
8. See Butler 1995 for a cogent critique of the BBC's ideological, political and institutional difficulties in broadcasting to Northern Ireland's 'divided community'.

Chapter 5

Representing 'Ordinary People' and Politics

In the previous chapter, we showed how the process of 'housetraining' the paramilitaries began with the Northern Ireland Office (NIO) advertisements for the confidential telephone. In what were in effect short films, paramilitaries were depicted as family men and women with a 'human face', instead of the monstrous pariahs of previous official propaganda. It was a public indication of how the British government's attitude to paramilitaries and their representatives was changing, for if previously violent individuals could be seen as people with families then their inclusion in the democratic process was easier to countenance.

While ascribing the virtues of domesticity to paramilitaries and their supporters has facilitated their entry into the mainstream of politics, attributing similar ideas to non-combatants has generally only served to present them as estranged from politics altogether. This is the category of 'ordinary people', who by definition are usually precluded from the media frame or at least marginalised in public and political discourse. They are an entirely constructed category; rarely permitted serious political convictions and motivations, and distinguished by their passive, domesticated citizenship.

BBC Radio Ulster's *Legacy* is an exemplar of this. Broadcast in 1999, it took the shape of a series of two-minute testimonies by 'the people of Northern Ireland and beyond [...] of the very human impact the violence has had on their lives'.[1] For Paul Moore (2003) this is an example of 'fourth phase public service broadcasting' in Northern Ireland, where notions of consensus and balanced sectarianism have outlived their usefulness. Moore detects instead a new, subject-focused approach that allows individuals to produce their own narratives about the troubles. Like the Ulster Museum's *Conflict: the Irish at War*, with its selected contributions from the public, *Legacy* offers a personalised version of the past. At the same time, however, its explicit emphasis on the 'human impact' of violence works to disallow not only the political perspectives and allegiances that lie at the heart of the conflict, but any political engagement other than a vague, liberal humanism.

There is no question that political violence in Northern Ireland has had personal, emotional and psychological repercussions (see, for example, Cairns et al 1995; or Muldoon 2004) but the preference for individualised understandings of, and perspectives on, the conflict should be seen in the broader context of the modernising, neo-liberal project that attended the peace process. As David Harvey points out, this is 'a world in which the neo-liberal ethic of intense, possessive individualism, and its political withdrawal from collective forms of action, becomes the template for human socialization' (Harvey 2008: 31).

A predilection for this sort of individualism and political abstention is explicit in the film *Divorcing Jack* (Caffrey 1998), based on the novel of the same name by Colin Bateman. It presents the political sphere as universally dystopian and wholly hostile to the interests of the individual. As a consequence, it advocates a withdrawal into domestic intimacy, demonstrated figuratively in a conversation between its protagonist Dan Starkey and a journalist colleague from the United States. The American asks Starkey what he prefers to call Northern Ireland: 'Ulster', 'the occupied six counties', 'the North' or 'the province'. Starkey tells him he just calls it 'home', avoiding the political and sectarian associations of the other designations. It is fitting then that most of the film is taken up with Starkey's efforts to rescue his private life after an act of marital infidelity plunges him into the world of political machinations, estranges him from his wife and leads to her kidnap by a renegade paramilitary.

The climactic scene finds Starkey caught between a duplicitous politician and an unreconstructed paramilitary. He berates them for their cynical disregard for individuals, whom he defines as people able to think for themselves, go for a pint with the lads and give 'the best fucking kiss in the world goodnight'. A similar romantic intimacy is emphasised in the final scene in which Starkey and his wife are reconciled at home and make love on what he describes as the 'magic settee'. Zavarzadeh refers to such a moment as one of 'plentitude, presence, and pellucidity: an instant in which the intimates are free from the mediating forces of culture and society and directly present to each other's consciousness, feelings, and perhaps bodies' (Zavarzadeh 1991:115). Zavarzadeh argues that such intimacy naturalises the notion of pan-historical and sovereign individuality, essential to contemporary capitalism. In this respect, the Starkeys' romantic intimacy transcends Northern Ireland's troublesome history and politics, while its location in the home shelters them from the political maelstrom beyond their front door. It also serves as a symbol of their political neutrality and the possessive individualism of the privatised and propertied neo-liberal subject.

Divorcing Jack is typical of most films and television dramas of the period in so far as politics is presented as a diametric threat to the domestic intimacies of 'ordinary people'. While such a perspective is understandable given Northern Ireland's history of sectarian violence, it has its negative consequences. Firstly, it assumes that the domestic sphere is unproblematic and free of politics, a notion that feminists would rightly dispute; and, secondly, it presents the political sphere, with its collective organisation and political struggle, as a universally hostile environment for 'ordinary people' whose proper place is at home. This atomised domesticity is, of course, ideologically conducive to the neo-liberal agenda that underscores the peace process and most often underwrites stories of embattled mothers, weak or conflicted fathers and innocent children.

Mothers

In film and television dramas such as *Holy Cross* (Brozel 2003), *Titanic Town* (Michell 1998) and *Some Mother's Son* (George 1996), domestic stability and political activism are incompatible as the mothers at the centre of these stories discover. *Holy Cross* dramatises the dispute between loyalists and nationalists in north Belfast throughout 2001. During this time loyalists from the Glenbryn housing estate in north Belfast picketed the entrance of a Catholic primary school, protesting at what they saw as the incursion into their area by neighbouring nationalists. Sarah Norton and Ann McClure are mothers from opposite sides of the sectarian divide whose houses stand back-to-back. However, despite being neighbours neither woman has ever spoken to the other and at a community meeting called to try to end the nightly sectarian violence in the area, they recognise each other but cannot bear to make eye contact. This sense of social division is emphasised in the drama by the women occupying essentially separate narratives that come together only through the conflict into which each of them is reluctantly drawn.

Sarah's eventual participation in the loyalist protest at the gates of the Holy Cross school is precipitated by the violence on her doorstep that leads to her best friend fleeing the area, leaving Sarah's house the only one still occupied on the 'frontline'. The final straw comes when, in the chaos of the protest, she loses her daughter behind police and army lines. Stressed, frustrated and vulnerable, the motivation behind her joining the protest has more to do with her fragile emotional state than genuine political conviction.

Ann, on the other hand, initially supports her husband, Gerry, a republican ex-prisoner, for whom the free passage of his children to school is a point of principle. However, when the protest escalates, Ann baulks at putting the children at risk by having them run the gauntlet of loyalist protestors for the sake of political principle. From that point onwards, her relationship with Gerry begins to deteriorate. It is a clash of irreconcilable political and domestic values articulated most effectively in one scene where she shouts at him: 'I would really like to talk to Gerry McClure the father, not Gerry McClure the voice of the people'. Ultimately, the repercussions of the conflict are felt in both homes. Ann and Gerry separate while Sarah's participation in the school picket jeopardises her relationship with her daughter Karen.

It is not just malevolent sectarian behaviour that impinges upon family life in these films. In *Titanic Town*, a mother's attempt to bring about the cessation of such violence puts a similar strain on her family relations. Set in the early 1970s but released, significantly, in the year of the Good Friday Agreement, the film tells the story of Bernie McPhelimy, a housewife who is concerned to protect her home and family from the encroaching violence in her neighbourhood. She attempts to broker a ceasefire between the IRA and British soldiers but ends up putting her own life and those of her family in greater danger.

Bernie's chief rival in the film is a slatternly, foul-mouthed republican neighbour who threatens Bernie and her family because of her involvement in the peace campaign. The contrast between the two women is striking. Bernie is conceived of as the custodian of womanly decorum in the film; a conscientious housekeeper – dignified, humble and selfless in her commitment to her family and determined to sustain its domestic integrity in the face of growing adversity. When the British Army carries out a series of house raids in the district, Bernie frets that the soldiers might enter her home to find the beds unmade and the children still in their nightclothes. This homely propriety is charming and comic, serving to elicit the empathy of the audience. Meanwhile, out on the street, her republican neighbour protests against the raids, shouting obscenities and shaking her fist at the soldiers. It is an indecorous and charmless performance that underlines the film's aversion to partisan politics and its preference for Bernie's domestic instincts. Indeed, the film re-emphasises this preference in each scene where the two women meet, most notably in an early confrontation at a public meeting called to discuss local concerns about the rising tensions in the area. Bernie follows protocol and addresses the meeting through the chair. She is polite, diffident and evidently modest. Her republican neighbour, on the other hand, makes a dramatic entrance at the head of an angry mob and denounces the participants for 'selling out' to the British.

In the end, however, Bernie's best efforts are undone not just by the violent attacks on her home and family initiated by her republican neighbour but by duplicity and politicking on both sides of the sectarian divide. Eventually, she is forced to stand down from the peace movement and leave her home and neighbourhood. As much as *Titanic Town* lauds the domestic virtues and instincts that inspired Bernie's campaign for peace, it nonetheless poses the political sphere as being diametrically opposed and threatening to the domestic and thus can find no place for the 'homely' Bernie in public life. Bernie is gratifyingly righteous but that righteousness is seemingly dependent upon her remaining politically powerless.

A similar retreat from the apparently insensible world of politics is evident in *Some Mother's Son*. The film is based upon the republican prisoners' dirty protest and subsequent hunger strike in 1981. While its characters are mostly fictional, it includes the depiction of some actual figures such as Bobby Sands, the first prisoner to die on that protest. The principal character in the film is Kathleen Quigley, a hitherto politically disinterested, Catholic teacher, who is drawn into the political sphere by necessity – the participation of her son in the hunger strike.

In the course of the film, Kathleen befriends Annie Higgins, a republican, whose son is also on strike. While the women differ radically in social class and political outlook, they bond in their shared determination to avert the deaths of their sons. To this end, they travel together to London to lobby British government officials, one of whom informs them that 'if your sons should lapse into comas, you have the legal right to take them off the strike', adding with mock poignancy, 'Surely no mother would allow her son to die?'

This arch politicking by the British government shifts the burden of responsibility to the mothers, irrespective of their sons' political commitment to the hunger strike. However, as we see in the film's denouement, Kathleen's political indifference empowers her to rise above the dispute and take action as both moral individual and mother. This is symbolised in a scene towards the end when she is party to an angry confrontation between mediator, Father Daly, and republican politician, Danny Boyle. The priest arrives at the prison and delivers to Boyle the terms upon which the British will settle the dispute: prisoners will be entitled to wear civilian clothing only as a 'privilege' rather than by 'right' as the prisoners demanded. For Boyle, it is a betrayal of trust on the part of the British government but Father Daly sees it as the best deal they can get and one that must be accepted to save lives. The argument seems to recall similar disputes over language, meaning and interpretation that have sometimes underscored the conflict and bedevilled attempts to find a settlement.

Kathleen is certainly repelled by such apparent pedantry and we see her leave the scene in slow motion, the raised voices of the priest and the politician distorted and indistinct – cinematic effects that emphasise her retreat from the political sphere. As she goes to the prison hospital and signs the form that takes her son off the strike and saves his life, Annie's son passes away in the next ward. When the two women meet outside on the corridor, Annie accepts Kathleen's offers of comfort and condolence and does not blame or reproach her for taking the action she did.

As a cinematic representation of life in Northern Ireland during the hunger strike – a critical, defining moment in the conflict – *Some Mother's Son* overrides the political and historical complexity of the dispute, preferring instead to use it as a theatrical backdrop against which to play out a simplistic moral drama. It throws its hero, Kathleen, into a political sphere that is occupied by two-dimensional stereotypes, and is a hostile space with little room or sympathy for family and private intimacies as represented by her love for her son. Even Annie, with her republican convictions, understands and appreciates this much but that does not absolve her from the moral indictment that the film delivers. While Kathleen is liberated by her refusal of politics, Annie is shackled by her political commitment, unable to act upon maternal instinct and save her son.

Fathers

In *Omagh* (Travis 2004) 'ordinary people' are pitched against similarly despicable politicians, paramilitaries and public authorities to those in *Titanic Town* and *Some Mother's Son*. The drama recalls the events of 15 August 1998, when the Real IRA detonated a car bomb in the market town of Omagh, killing 31 people. Among the dead was Aiden Gallagher, the teenage son of Michael Gallagher, a self-employed car mechanic who eventually emerged as a leading spokesperson for the Omagh Support and Self Help Group, an association of victims' families whose campaign in search of truth and justice helped to uncover official negligence and subterfuge surrounding the bombing. Focusing on a grieving father, in the figure of Michael Gallagher, *Omagh* is less concerned to make the retreat from public activism as emphatic as the mothers' in *Holy Cross*, *Titanic Town* and *Some Mother's Son*. This is clear when Michael's involvement in the self help group's campaign is vindicated at the end when the Police Ombudsman, Nuala O'Loan, delivers a damning verdict on the performance of the police at a press conference, confirming the group's suspicions. Afterwards Michael makes a statement to the media and leaves flanked by his wife and two daughters, in a scene that assures the audience that public activism and domestic stability are not necessarily inimical. However, Michael's family life does not go untested by his involvement in the campaign. His wife withdraws both from him and the campaign, and his youngest daughter reproaches him for neglecting his fatherly responsibilities. This sequence is immediately followed by a poignant shot of Michael in the self help group mini-bus, en route to meet Royal Ulster Constabulary chief constable Ronnie Flanagan. There is a vacant seat beside him that was previously occupied by his wife. The meeting with Flanagan is a disappointment and the group returns to Omagh demoralised and exhausted, with even Michael vowing to 'stay home'. However he re-emerges into public life when the Police Ombudsman delivers her report. Michael tells his wife that he is going to the press conference to 'show some solidarity'.

Evidence of solidarity in Northern Ireland on screen is rare. Mothers like Bernie McPhelimy, Sarah Norton, Ann McClure and Kathleen Quigley are depicted as embattled individuals, besieged by intemperate political convictions and/or torn between public activism and domestic duties. Michael Gallagher, on the other hand, is connected to a community, demonstrated initially by his familiarity with, and knowledge of, many of the other victims and their families, and further established by his involvement with the self help group. When he intervenes at the first public meeting called by the victims' families it offers an interesting contrast with Bernie McPhelimy's reluctant contribution to a meeting of concerned local residents in *Titanic Town*. Bernie and Michael are played as unpretentious characters, a prerequisite to their ordinariness, but whereas Bernie is charming and naïve, often to comic effect, Michael is eloquent, authoritative and sombre. His demeanour galvanises the meeting and establishes the collective terms upon which the families can progress their cause. By contrast, Bernie is easily usurped by her aggressive republican neighbour, a weakness that presages her eventual loss of political agency. In *Omagh*, political agency is explicitly linked to solidarity. As Michael tells the self help group at its rowdy inaugural meeting, they will get nowhere if they do not work together. His intervention brings calm and silences the fractious, individual voices that greeted him when he first entered the room. In this way *Omagh* goes some way to vindicating solidarity and public activism. Not so *Holy Cross* or *Titanic Town*, where any form of community or social solidarity seems potentially dangerous, to the extent that in *Holy Cross*, the initially moribund Glenbryn Residents Association is energised by the initiation of the loyalist picket at the school and becomes a vehicle for angry, uncompromising voices.

Omagh's complimentary depiction of a campaigning father is not typical of film and television dramas about Northern Ireland in this period, most of which depict fathers and other adult males as weak, feckless, immature or dangerous. For instance, Bernie McPhelimy's husband in *Titanic Town* and Victor Kelly's father in *Resurrection Man* are presented as weak and ailing characters, failing to provide a patriarchal and moderating influence on wives and children. The loyalist men in *Nothing Personal* and *Resurrection Man* seem wed to violence. However, while republican men have tended to fair better recently, being represented as increasingly responsible, domesticated citizens, in *Holy Cross*, Gerry McClure's strong political convictions are presented as a problem and leave him estranged from his family. In this respect his portrayal contrasts with the representation of Michael Gallagher, whose ambition to seek truth and justice through the cross-community self help group apparently transcends the partisan politics represented by Gerry McClure's republicanism.

In addition to weak and partisan fathers there is a selection of socially immature 'uncles', usually associated with loyalism, whose inclusion in the immediate family is a source of anxiety and grief. These include Freddie in *As the Beast Sleeps* (Bradbeer 2002) and, in *Holy Cross*, Sarah Norton's live-in brother, Peter, whose peccant immaturity is contrasted with the virtuous innocence of his young niece, Karen. The representation of children like Karen in Northern Ireland on screen is what we look at next.

Children

Children motivate the politically disinterested mothers and fathers of Northern Ireland on screen to move into roles of public activism, and it is usually in the interests of those children that the parents return to domestic duties, turning their backs on the world of politics. Children themselves are often represented as prelapsarian; associated with nature rather than the contested social world; or they provide a means by which to view adult behaviour askance.

In *Holy Cross*, viewing the world of grown-ups from the perspective of a child offers a salutary comment on the apparent grotesqueness of sectarianism as well as other adult frailties. This child's-eye view on the world is quite literal in the case of Sarah's daughter Karen, who is compiling a video diary for a school project. This device serves to introduce us to Karen, her family and home, all of which are presented through the viewfinder of a domestic camcorder, as in one poignant moment when she asks her feckless uncle Peter, 'What do you want to be when you grow up?' His discomfiture at this inquiry is in part what motivates him to become involved in the loyalist protests at the school gates, giving his otherwise directionless life some purpose. Similarly, it is from Karen's perspective that we see her mother's eventual involvement in the loyalist picket, haranguing the Catholic schoolchildren and their parents. This sequence from Karen's point of view is shot in slow motion, the raised voices of the other protestors fading out to leave only Sarah repeatedly screaming 'scum' at her Catholic neighbours. These visual and audio effects simultaneously isolate Sarah and give expression to Karen's sense of alienation from her mother, who has succumbed to the very sectarianism for which she earlier scolded her daughter. It is only when Sarah returns her daughter's gaze with a direct look to camera that the expressionist mask of rage falls from her face. As with Uncle Peter's self-realisation of his own futility, the inference and invitation is clear: it is through the child's eyes that Northern Ireland should come to know itself, a gaze that exposes the monstrousness of sectarianism.

The romantic, prelapsarian conception of childhood is also evident in *Mickybo and Me* (Loane 2004), a rite-of-passage buddy movie about two friends, Mickybo and Jonjo, from either side of Belfast's sectarian divide in the early 1970s. Modelling themselves on their screen idols, Butch Cassidy and the Sundance Kid, the two go on the run, in the mistaken belief that they have shot an elderly neighbour dead in his bath with a gun found in his house. Pursued by the law and reported by the media, the boys live out their 'outlaw' dream unaware that in a real sense their cross-community friendship makes them 'outlaws' from the sectarian society in which they are growing up.

Determined to escape to Australia, as their on-screen heroes had intended to do, the boys head south looking for a boat and leap off a pier into the sea to avoid capture by the police. As the boys jump they are caught in freeze-frame, suspended in mid-air, holding out the tantalising possibility of arresting time and denying the subsequent history of violence and sectarian recriminations. But of course there is no plausible means of escape, either from the police or the sectarianism and violence that awaits them on their return to Belfast. Once captured and returned home Mickybo discovers that loyalists have murdered his father and the boys' friendship disintegrates.

Mickybo starts to run with the sectarian youths he once defended Jonjo from and as if to prove his sectarian credentials to his new comrades he stabs Jonjo outside the cinema where the they found friendship in the outlaw fantasies of the Western. Now showing is *Dracula*, a shift in genre that alludes to the change in the boys' lives and environment. It also offers a context within which to regard the image of Jonjo's blood on the knife's blade. The bloodied weapon recalls the boyish ceremony performed by Mickybo when he declared Jonjo and himself 'blood brothers'.

That familial oath is recalled at the end of film. Mickybo, now an adult, is resident in Cassidy's Bar, where his father was shot dead 30 years previously. He is last pictured in the twilight gloom of the public house, sitting where his dead father was last seen slumped on the bar. The implication is clear: Mickybo has not moved on from his traumatic introduction to sectarianism. However Jonjo, it seems, has and he writes to Mickybo from Australia where he now lives, enclosing a photograph of his family in Sydney, a symbol of his progress into constitutional adulthood. Significantly the accompanying letter holds out the possibility of reconciliation as Jonjo reminisces and recalls the childish oath they took to be 'blood brothers'. The film closes with a close-up of Mickybo's face fading to a shot of the two boys leaping off the pier. As John Hill argues, the film's attempt to hold onto a moment of 'prelapsarian glee' in this way is 'eloquently symptomatic of the problems involved in trying to turn the "troubles" into a crowd-pleasing entertainment' (Hill 2006: 243).

The Mighty Celt (Elliot 2005) has a more optimistic ending than *Mickybo and Me*. It is a coming-of-age film about a young boy called Donal who works most of his spare time for a local greyhound trainer called Good Joe. Despite his name, Joe treats his dogs with cruelty, a sin compounded by his duplicity and his continued commitment to violent republicanism. Donal on the other hand is an innocent who persuades Joe to invest in the eponymous greyhound despite the man's doubts about the dog's racing pedigree. In contrast to Joe, Donal has a strong emotional attachment to the dogs and this quality is integral to his successful training of the Mighty Celt, which he undertakes on his own and without recourse to the brutal techniques of his employer. The contrast between man and boy is further emphasised when Donal releases the rabbits that Joe had planned to feed alive to his dogs. His affiliation with animals, coupled with sequences of him training and playing with the Mighty Celt in the hills and countryside around Belfast, associate him with nature as opposed to the conflicted social world of the city and Joe's militant republican politics. It is Donal's innocence that is at stake in his relationship with Joe, under whose nefarious influence he has fallen. Here the film introduces a counterpoint to Joe in the shape of O, an IRA man whose return to Belfast after years on the run is made possible by the new dispensation.

Like Danny in *The Boxer*, O is the image of domesticated republicanism. A sequence of him doing housework in tiger-feet slippers is complemented by the revelation that he has a taste for classical music and is concerned about his weight, which prompts Donal to describe him as the 'funniest' IRA man he has ever seen on account of him not being sufficiently 'big and ugly'. For O, his return is the opportunity to rekindle a romantic relationship with Kate, Donal's typically embattled mother. She describes herself as both 'victim and survivor' of the troubles and she resents O's 'gallivanting' while she was confined to a housing estate looking after her child, excluded from the 'experiences' and freedom she presumes he enjoyed on the run. The reason for her disapprobation becomes clearer when it transpires that O is Donal's biological father but this is a role that he is required to prove himself fit for, competing with Good Joe for influence over his son. In the end, he peacefully separates Donal and Joe, sets up home with Kate and secures for Donal the sort of domestic intimacies that preserve the innocence that Joe endangered.

The preservation of childhood innocence is at the heart of *The Most Fertile Man in Ireland* (Appleton 1999), which forgoes the realism of *The Mighty Celt* and *Mickybo and Me*, preferring instead visual excess, gross comedy and romance. The lead character is bachelor, Eamonn Manley, whose extraordinary sperm opens up an excellent business opportunity: to exploit a crisis in male fertility that the film imagines some time in the future. He offers his services to childless couples for money but the promiscuity that this new career necessarily entails threatens his fledgling romance with Rosie. However, retirement is out of the question since his fertility has brought him to the attention of competing Protestant and Catholic leaders, determined to enlist his help to out-breed each other. But Eamonn rejects their unwelcome advances and, by implication, the sectarian labelling of his many children, insisting that he has bred 'faithless little Eamonns'. In the end he has a vasectomy, an operation that renders him of no political consequence. Free from the attentions of loyalists and nationalists, Eamonn joins Rosie and their newborn twins in hospital, a scene that emphasises the film's preference for what Raymond Williams refers to as 'retreating privatisation' (quoted in Hill 2006: 228). This is given symbolic emphasis in the final sequence when Eamonn and Rosie are pictured against a white backdrop – a symbolic blank canvas – surrounded by all the children that Eamonn has fathered. As Hill argues, this presents the characters in an abstract way, 'detached from any particular time or place'. He says: '[T]he film seems to pluck its couple from the specific political context with which they were previously associated and celebrates their successful escape into the privatised – and universalised – sphere of the family unit' (Hill 2006: 228).

In another way, the scene is comparable to the NIO advertisement, *Northern Irish Difference* (NIO 1995), which sought to encourage cross-community cooperation through the depiction of children playing in a crèche, while making the point that Protestant and Catholic children are indistinguishable. In *The Most Fertile Man in Ireland* the children's neutrality seems assured by their location in a semiotic and political limbo.

Entrepreneurs

However, one of the striking contradictions at the heart of *The Most Fertile Man in Ireland* is that it mocks the very enterprise culture that its vision of 'retreating privatisation' depends upon. In its version of entrepreneurial Northern Ireland, romance offers a business opportunity, exploited by the Amoré dating agency where Eamonn works. This entrepreneurial spirit is encapsulated by Millicent, Amoré's 'marketing trainee of the month'. Not surprisingly then it is she who sees the profitable potential in Eamonn's 'gift', acts as his agent and describes him as a 'one man service industry'. Yet it is this very same enterprise (tied to notions of male virility) that Eamonn has to give up if he wants to secure real love. Pivotal to the film, therefore, are two versions of sexuality – one public and entrepreneurial, the other private and personal.

Entrepreneurship works rather differently in *An Everlasting Piece* (Levinson 2000), where Colm and George, Catholic and Protestant barbers, work in a grim mental hospital, surely an analogy for Northern Ireland. This is a place of insanity, where the patients are overwhelmingly Catholic, the staff is dominated by dour Protestants and the most dangerous inmate is a Bible-bashing fundamentalist known as 'the Scalper'. Its depressing representation of the public sector also seems to recall Bob Rowthorn's description of Northern Ireland as a 'workhouse economy' (Rowthorn 1987: 117) where most people are either involved in the administration or policing of one another. Indeed, the mental hospital in *An Everlasting Piece* resembles nothing so much as an old Victorian workhouse, many of which were converted into hospitals with the introduction of the welfare state. Resolved to escape this environment, Colm and George try to win a franchise to sell hair-pieces in Northern Ireland, encountering challenges from balding loyalists and republicans. In the penultimate scene of the film, the camera pans down over Belfast City Hall and its environs, picturesquely illuminated by Christmas lights, and moves in on the exterior of a small pub. Inside, the camera pans over the heads of its happy patrons until it finds George, Colm and his girlfriend, Bronagh, celebrating their business success in a way that proffers entrepreneurship as the apparent basis of cross-community accord and the social invigoration of Belfast.

More satirically scathing about the enterprising pretensions of Northern Ireland is *Eureka Street* (BBC Northern Ireland 1999), a series of four, one-hour episodes broadcast in 1999 and based on Robert McLiam Wilson's novel of the same name. While engaging with themes of forgiveness and redemption, *Eureka Street* also pokes satirical fun at sanctimonious republicans and apocalyptic loyalists. However, it reserves special attention to the rebranding of Northern Ireland in the global market.

The story follows the fortunes of Jake Jackson, a hard-boiled cynic and repo-man who is trying to come to terms with a failed love affair. As an orphan brought up by foster parents, Jake is an outsider, without religious or political conviction save for his acerbic rejection of his Irish nationalist background. He introduces us to Chuckie Lurgan, his best friend, 'a fat Prod' from Eureka Street, who at 30 is unemployed and still living at home with his mother,

Peggy. Chuckie's social immaturity and cherub-like appearance mark him as a 'child', a fact emphasised by him being first glimpsed in the childish domain of a sweetshop.

Eureka Street presents Belfast from Jake and Chuckie's misfit-perspectives, emphasised in the visual style of the drama. Characters are seen in extreme close-ups that distort their features, or odd camera angles that render them askew. The city and its interiors are frequently rendered through an expressionist use of light and colour. The overall effect is to present Belfast and its inhabitants as slightly out of kilter with the 'real' world, its uniqueness established in the sentiments of Jake Jackson's introduction were he points out to the viewer that:

> Under the circumstances Belfast is a pretty famous place. I mean, when you consider that it's the under-populated capital of a minor province the world seems to know it pretty well. […] Belfast shares the status of the battlefield. Belfast is big because Belfast is bad.

However, Belfast is also a city striving to find its place in global capitalism and in *Eureka Street* its efforts are mocked through the incongruous notion that a 'fat Prod' like Chuckie, an immature loser, can become an entrepreneurial success. First of all he advertises sex toys of which he has no stock, making money from customers too embarrassed to demand a refund when they do not receive the merchandise. Then he convinces the Ulster Development Board to award him £1.2 million, when by his own admission he neither makes nor sells anything. He teams up with obsequious financial consultant, Luke Findlaker, who considers Chuckie's ability to make money out of nothing a sign of his entrepreneurial genius. Under his tutelage Chuckie markets 'the very best Northern Ireland has to offer' with a series of crass and improbable products, including an ecumenical dating agency, leprechaun walking sticks and paramilitary balaclavas, which he describes as the 'ultimate fashion statement on the ski slopes of Colorado'. However Chuckie's financial good fortune contrasts sharply with events in his private life. He falls in love with, and then loses, a beautiful but troubled young American woman called Max, while his mother is badly traumatised in a bomb explosion. In an attempt to help her recover, Chuckie buys her a lorry-load of domestic appliances that won't fit into her small terrace house. The gesture is excessive and seems an ironic comment on Jake's profession as a repo-man, which is to empty homes of unpaid-for household goods. In any case Chuckie's hyper-consumerism has no impact on his mother's health but she begins to improve and finds a new lease of life when she beings a love affair with her long-time best friend Caroline.

Chuckie finds his mother's lesbian love life hard to come to terms with but the broad message of *Eureka Street* is that happiness and fulfilment are found in romantic success. The opening sequence of the first episode is of a single sentence typed slowly onto a page: 'All stories are love stories'. Chuckie learns this when he catches up with Max and confesses to her that all his life he thought 'something was missing' and that all he needed was fame and riches when all the time what he really needed was her. The realisation is a step on the way to Chuckie's growing maturity, which culminates in his acceptance of his mother's lesbian relationship. For Max's part, her relationship with Chuckie is redemptive. She has been 'fucking and running' since the assassination of her father, a US diplomat, in Ireland.

Jake also finds redemptive love with Aoirghe, a bitter republican whose relationship with him is initially antagonistic. Jake is cynical about politics and scathing about the cultural expression of Irish nationalism, which Aoirghe interprets as evident self-loathing. Her bitterness, like Max's promiscuity, lies in a childhood trauma associated with the conflict in Ireland. She witnessed her father being crippled by a British soldier during a raid on her family's home. In a sense, *Eureka Street*, peopled by the orphaned, the socially immature and the traumatised, seems to offer some sort of metaphorical comment on Belfast.

We might think of this in relation to Martin McLoone's (2000) perceptive analysis of *The Butcher Boy* (Jordan 1997). He proposes a possible political reading of the film in which he sees its leading character, Francie Brady, as the 'abused child of Irish history', a metaphor that 'symbolises the great abuse that the Irish people have suffered, from colonisation generally but from the Famine and emigration in particular' (McLoone 2000: 219–220). *Eureka Street* has its own ebullient urchin, the one genuine child of note in the series, Roche, who sells newspapers and tells jokes in pubs for 10p a time to get by. He is the product of an evidently abusive home and broader social failures are alluded to through his illiteracy and absence from school. He is nevertheless resourceful but the full measure of his vulnerability becomes clear when he is hospitalised by republicans who subject him to a vicious punishment beating.

The incident serves to confront Aoirghe with the implications of her vocal support for violent republicanism, while Jake is made to face what are perhaps the consequences of his own cynical detachment but almost certainly his failure to act as a proper 'father' to the boy he befriended and sheltered. Roche's beating is the catalyst that lays the ground for a romantic rapprochement between Aoirghe and Jake.

Eureka Street never makes clear what becomes of Roche. He is last seen lying in the accident and emergency ward of a Belfast hospital and he is never referred to again. On the one hand, it might appear that he is reduced to little more than a MacGuffin, used to facilitate Jake and Aoirghe's romantic union; on the other hand, seen in metaphorical terms, the uncertainty about his fate is a comment on the condition of Belfast itself. In this context, the coupling of Chuckie and Max, Jake and Aoirghe, and Chuckie's mother and Caroline offers closure and resolution to private lives only. Political questions are left open.

The series seeks to make a virtue of this openness when Chuckie's interests expand into politics. On a late-night news programme, he berates Northern Ireland's politicians but his parody of Martin Luther King's 'I have a dream' speech renders his political intervention a caricature. Even the political party that Chuckie forms after the news broadcast has little substance. He calls it the OTG, an acronym that has been mysteriously daubed on walls all around Belfast. However, Chuckie confesses he doesn't know what he is doing or what OTG stands for. Jake assures him that this is of little consequence when seen in the context of all the other political acronyms on Belfast's walls – IRA, UDA, UVF, INLA.

The great lazy majority would never be arsed writing anything anywhere or they wouldn't know what to write or they'd change their minds halfway through. OTG was written for them because it could mean anything they wanted.

The 'tyrannies of intimacy'

If as David Butler suggests, in Northern Ireland all the signifiers are spoken for by one political persuasion or another (Butler 1995: 135), then *Eureka Street*'s empty signifier, 'OTG', offers some respite in the crowded marketplace of loaded political acronyms. The problem for *Eureka Street* is that Northern Ireland's 'great lazy majority' make their preference for sectarian designations clear at each election. Like all other dramatic attempts to try to present 'ordinary people' as somehow politically disinterested, neutral or lazy, *Eureka Street* comes up against the fact that 'ordinary people' in Northern Ireland have political preferences and dispositions and they don't mind expressing them in a variety of ways – some constitutional and democratic, others less so. As a consequence most film and television drama seeks consolation in a humanism that transcends the political and historical, manifesting itself in the universal signifiers of romantic encounters and family life. Just how embedded this way of representing Northern Ireland has become was made clear in a television interview immediately after the broadcast of *Holy Cross*, with its screenwriter, Terry Cafolla. During the interview Cafolla claimed that in writing *Holy Cross* he had tried to 'forget about the political circumstances' and concentrate on the 'personal dilemmas' facing the two families in the drama.[2] Yet how (or indeed why) would anyone make a drama out of events in north Belfast over the summer of 2001, when loyalists picketed a Catholic primary school, and try to forget the political circumstances? Yet the elision of politics in contemporary Northern Ireland on screen is routine and, as a consequence, anyone with political convictions is generally represented as deviant and/or incomprehensible to so-called 'ordinary people'. This can only have the effect of mystifying rather than clarifying any understanding of political conflict and public life, a condition not exclusive to Northern Ireland.

In his book *The Fall of Public Man*, Richard Sennett considers how an obsession with the self, personality and intimate human relations in western culture has led to a withdrawal from political and public life. He argues that we now consider public matters more in terms of personal feelings and intimate relations than through 'codes of impersonal meaning' (Sennett 1977: 5). Able only to see public concerns in private terms we have lost much or our rational understanding of society. This, Sennett argues, leaves us ill-prepared to think about the forces of domination and inequality (Sennett 1977: 339). Such a shrinking of public culture is a consequence of social change in the nineteenth century that saw the arrival of a mass-produced, consumer culture that encouraged passivity in public and the rise of a secular society that privileged the immanent over the transcendent. In the upheavals that attended these changes, the family emerged as both refuge from the terrors of society and a 'moral yardstick with which to measure the public realm' (Sennett 1977: 20).

Making Northern Ireland comprehensible to the 'civilised world' (evoked by Tony Blair in July 1999) has been a process of subjecting it to what Sennett calls the 'tyrannies of intimacy'; or as we see it here, the pacification of public life through privatisation and domestication. Film and television dramas have ideologically prepared the ground for this with stories of domesticated republicans and embattled individuals struggling to secure their homes and families against an unvaryingly adverse political and public sphere.

Notes

1. BBC (n.d.), 'Northern Ireland: The Troubles – Legacy', http://www.bbc.co.uk/history/recent/troubles/legacy.shtml. Accessed 19 August 2009.
2. Terry Cafolla was interviewed on *The John Daly Show* immediately after the broadcast of his television drama *Holy Cross* on 10 November 2003 – BBC Northern Ireland (2003), *The John Daly Show*.

Chapter 6

No Alternative Ulster

The propaganda of peace, as defined and identified in this book, has been reproduced in different media and cultural forms, supported and sponsored by various political, social and cultural agencies. Nevertheless, it has demonstrated a remarkable unity, narrowing the terms of political debate and shrinking the cultural imagination to promote two complimentary narratives about Northern Ireland's bright new future. The first, most explicit and immediate narrative was about the need for an end to violence and the achievement of a political settlement between Catholic and Protestant, nationalist and unionist. The second, implicit and far-reaching narrative was about making Northern Ireland fit for integration into the global capitalist system or, as Tony Blair preferred to call it, the 'civilised world'. Before we consider the explanatory and persuasive power of each and assess their critical implications, we will first address the concept of the propaganda of peace as a theoretical problem.

The propaganda of peace and the 'structure of feeling'

The key architects of the peace process and the Good Friday Agreement – the British and Irish governments along with the leading political parties in Northern Ireland – employed clearly defined propaganda tactics and strategies to promote via the mainstream news media their own particular versions of the settlement for their own particular ends. However, while the production and effects of this propaganda is in itself significant, our concern in this volume has been to work on a much less systematic, less conspiratorial conceptualisation of propaganda.

We wanted the reader to think of the propaganda of peace as a constellation of images and messages produced intuitively and informally by a diverse range of media and cultural forms at a particular political and cultural moment in history. Our problem was finding a theoretical or conceptual tool to help us explain the nature of this propaganda and to demonstrate the explicit and implicit levels on which it operated. Antonio Gramsci's conception of hegemony (Gramsci 1971) as an organic alliance of political and cultural agencies is a useful starting point but it does not help us explain how such an alliance might influence events and behaviour both deliberately and in a less self-conscious, ideological manner. Here we turn to Raymond Williams and his notion of a 'structure of feeling', which he defines as the 'felt sense of the quality of life at a particular time and place: a sense of the ways in which the particular activities combined into a way of thinking and living' (Williams 1961: 47). He elaborates on this later:

The point of the deliberately contradictory phrase […] is that it is a structure in the sense that you could perceive it operating in one work after another which weren't otherwise connected – people weren't learning it from each other; yet it was one of feeling much more than of thought – a pattern of impulses, restraints, tones, for which the best evidence was often the actual conventions of literary and dramatic writing. (Williams 1979: 159)

Williams himself was never entirely at ease with the concept but crucially, from our point of view, he kept coming back to it 'from the actual experience of literary analysis rather than from any theoretical satisfaction [with it]' (Williams 1979: 159). It seems to us that even allowing for its complications, the concept still packs considerable explanatory power when analysing the production of peace propaganda from such a diverse and not always connected range of media and cultural sources. It enables us to demonstrate the common themes and ideas that emerged during the peace process from news and journalism, museum exhibitions, film, television drama and situation comedy; and to show how these affirmed and underscored the explicit and implicit narratives of the propaganda of peace which, as a 'structure of feeling', lubricate in Williams' words 'the interaction between the official consciousness of an epoch…and the whole process of actually living its consequences' (Williams 1979: 159).

The explicit narrative: an end to violence and the achievement of a political settlement

We began our analysis by looking at news coverage, traditionally the media format preferred by 'official' sources for the communication of propaganda messages. Northern Ireland's local newspapers were all advocates of the peace process, following the government line and in some instances giving over front-page headlines to the pronouncements and endorsements of the British Prime Minister, Tony Blair. When, in the build-up to the referendum, Blair urged voters to ignore the 'naysayers', the local press helped his cause by marginalising the No campaign in their coverage. And in the wake of the result, they downplayed the significance of an evenly split Unionist vote in the interests of upholding the political accord they had greeted as 'historic'. But behind their upbeat support for peace and a political settlement lay a more troubling, editorial undertone. Throughout the referendum campaign, the Belfast dailies, especially and remarkably the unionist *News Letter* and *Belfast Telegraph*, couched their comments in the democratic rhetoric of the people's right to choose while at the same time making it clear that there was no alternative to voting Yes. However such a process cannot be democratic and foretold unless its politics are first denied.

Despite the media's unanimous approval, the political process progressed into the new century in a state of almost perpetual crisis. By the time the parties met at St Andrews in 2006 to try once more to cut a final deal, the British and Irish governments had run out of patience, a mood reflected in newspaper coverage of the talks. Politicians were encouraged to 'get on with it', revive devolved government and address the pressing 'bread and butter' issues of health, education, tax and water rates. With the 'eyes of the world' now turned elsewhere to conflicts such as Iraq and Afghanistan, Northern Ireland was strictly a domestic affair. Its peace process had fallen into some disrepute and nothing illustrated this more than the *Belfast Telegraph*'s editorial treatment of the St Andrews talks. The paper marked the beginning of the summit with the momentous headline 'Destiny Day' (*Belfast Telegraph* 10 April 1998) but quickly shifted tone, poking fun at the participants and comparing their efforts to movies such as *Groundhog Day* and *Back to the Future*. It was a far cry from the heightened sense of optimism and historic significance in the period of the Agreement and referendum, a mood engendered by the attention of the US President Bill Clinton, who intervened at key moments of the peace process and took time on the eve of the referendum to urge voters to say 'Yes'. Alluding to Seamus Heaney's play, *The Cure At Troy*, he said in a radio address that, 'The people of Northern Ireland have an opportunity to join hope to history'.[1] But the high historical watermark had been reached at that point: St Andrews was merely history repeating itself as farce.

Coincidentally, history was recruited for the ideological needs of the present in the Ulster Museum's *Up In Arms* exhibition in the summer of 1998. The attempts to achieve an 'agreed Ireland' in this, the bicentenary of the 1798 uprising, seemed to resonate with the United Irishmen's aspiration for a 'cordial union among all the people of Ireland'. The exhibition's linear and didactic account of the uprising affirmed the centrist, consensual ambitions of Northern Ireland's moderates and overlapped with the ideological work being performed by the newspapers in that both privileged the liberal, 'progressivist subject'. While *Up In Arms* conferred historical legitimacy upon this position in the present, news coverage of the Agreement and referendum confirmed that there would be 'no alternative' to it in the future. The message was clear: that to deviate from the progressivist narrative would be to consign Northern Ireland to what one newspaper called 'the wilderness of European history'. Other liberal strategies for dealing with conflict, such as centrism and balance, predate the peace process but the new dispensation allowed for a personalising and domesticating of politics and history that would have seemed impossible before the ceasefires – for example, the Ulster Museum's subjective accounts of the past in *Conflict: the Irish at War*. It is this very privileging of the subjective position that underwrites the other, implicit narrative that emerges out of the propaganda of peace: that of Northern Ireland and its future in the 'civilised world'.

The implicit narrative: Northern Ireland and the 'civilised world'

In news and current affairs, the BBC has demonstrated that existing liberal approaches could be complimented by the emerging domesticated sensibilities, suggesting that the new times did not necessarily mean an abandonment of previous representational strategies. A good example of this is *Talk Back*, BBC Radio Ulster's long-running current affairs programme, produced by Seamus Boyd, that has garnered a reputation for being unafraid to broadcast the most uncompromising and bigoted opinions. Each weekday, between noon and 1.30pm, its presenter, David Dunseith, encourages and provokes listeners to phone in, email or text their views on the news of the day and other 'burning issues'. In Northern Ireland, such an invitation invariably draws heated, sometimes sectarian, political debate on air. It also draws criticism from republicans and loyalists who regularly target their anger at *Talk Back*'s presenter and, by extension, the BBC. Unionist listeners berate the show for promoting a republican agenda, while nationalists attack its perceived unionist bias. Such criticism is by now routine but it completely misses the point. *Talk Back* is indeed biased but its political preferences are neither unionist nor nationalist. As befits a product of the BBC in Northern Ireland, the programme makes room for balanced sectarian comment but its conscience is determinedly centrist. The presenter often consoles himself on air with the notion that if *Talk Back* is attracting flak from 'both sides' in Northern Ireland then it must be 'doing something right', namely demonstrating its impartiality and balance. However, David Dunseith provides the programme with a paternal voice of reason and moderation; he is the personification of the BBC and its preference for consensual politics. Nevertheless, it has to be said that since Dunseith's arrival in the *Talk Back* chair the programme has been one of the few that has aired the sort of fractious voices that are probably more typical of Northern Ireland than the liberal sensibilities preferred by the BBC.

The peace process, however, has presented *Talk Back* with a dilemma: how to manage and reconcile these fractious voices with the new political and cultural dispensation of conflict resolution and transformation? The solution has been two-fold: to reduce hard political content in favour of a lighter, populist agenda and to foster the conception of programme and listeners as part of a 'family' in which conflict can be defused. In fact, when asked about how the programme managed a dispute with the then Grand Master of the Orange Order, Robert Saulters, the producer, Seamus Boyd, drew the analogy of a family row: '*Talk Back* is a bit like a family. There are fall-outs; people have a little bit of annoyance but then they'll come back some other day because we've annoyed somebody else instead and they like that'.[2]

On television, the process of domesticating and personalising Northern Ireland's politics began on the BBC's current affairs programme, *Hearts and Minds*. In the wake of the Agreement, it canvassed the public for their views on the personal presentation of Northern Ireland's Assembly members and invited them to name the best-dressed political representative. This was followed up in the studio with 'expert' evaluations from an image consultant and a local hairdresser.[3] In a subsequent broadcast, the programme interviewed the partners of local assembly members, gaining some insight into their personal relationships.[4]

Such human-interest content marked a departure from the 1980s, when situating Northern Ireland's combative politicians in the realms of the ordinary or the domestic was to say the least a risky proposition for public-service broadcasters. Indeed, it is worth recalling at this point the controversy surrounding *Real Lives*, 'At the Edge of the Union' (BBC 1985). As we showed in chapter 4, the programme's portrayal of Martin McGuinness incurred the wrath of the British government and the unionist establishment. Here was a man regarded as an IRA commander shown at home with his wife and family, carrying out his role as local councillor and going to church. It sat very uneasily with the anti-terrorist propaganda image of the armalite-toting, masked IRA man. Yet, looking back on the programme through the filter of the peace process and the apparent normalisation of life in Northern Ireland, it is the portrayal not of McGuinness but his arch-nemesis, Gregory Campbell of the Democratic Unionist Party that looks the most remarkable and offers up a striking irony. He is seen loading a handgun at home, a weapon issued to him by the police for defensive purposes. The scene underscores a rarefied domestic environment: an ordinary man in a modest terraced house but one fortified by extraordinary security measures such as armoured doors, steel window grilles and CCTV cameras.

In the context of all we have discussed in this book, about the propaganda of peace and how it has played its role in conflict transformation, it is possible to look on 'At the Edge of the Union' today and see the portrayal of Campbell as an aberration and that of McGuinness as the affirmation of the ordinary. It is also possible to see in their political careers the distance Northern Ireland has travelled from conflict to peace. At the time the programme was broadcast, both men were local councillors on opposite sides of the sectarian divide in Derry. By 2007, 22 years later, they had taken their places in the Northern Ireland Executive; McGuinness as Deputy First Minister, Campbell as Minister for Culture, Arts and Leisure. For liberal advocates of the peace process, it was a moment that vindicated the long struggle for compromise and parity of esteem in Northern Ireland's body politic. But as we shall see in more recent media representations, it is not the whole story. These reveal another strand to the story that is about settling Northern Ireland within global capitalism.

The image that apparently won the referendum in 1998 – Bono of U2, lifting the arms of David Trimble and John Hume in a gesture of triumphant reconciliation – seemed to encapsulate a moment in the peace process when all that the people had to do was say Yes and this vision of peace on stage would become reality for everyone on the ground. But there is another image we wish to present here that is less heroic, much more mundane but no less remarkable for that.

It is December 2007, nearly ten years since the signing of the Good Friday Agreement. Ian Paisley and Martin McGuinness, First Minister and Deputy First Minister of Northern Ireland respectively, come to the opening of IKEA's new furniture superstore in Belfast. They sit for a photo opportunity on an IKEA sofa, relaxed and smiling, an image framed by the corporate slogan in the background: 'Home is the most important place in the world'. The triumphalism of Trimble and Hume's Bono moment is superseded by the banality of Paisley and McGuinness's IKEA moment: here they were now, leaders of once militant republicanism and truculent loyalism, pacified and domesticated, endorsing a determinedly apolitical and nakedly consumerist brand identity. In a sense these two images bookend the ideological meaning of the peace process and expose its pretensions and limitations: how the 'historic' achievement of political accord gave way to the modest realisation of a 'peace dividend' and Northern Ireland's integration into the consumerist society and the global economic order.

Paisley-McGuinness at Ikea Belfast. Pacemaker Press International Ltd

As part of the media narrative of the peace process, the 'peace dividend' is one widely celebrated but barely questioned in public debate. Just after the signing of the Good Friday Agreement, the *Belfast Telegraph* reported that 'US President Bill Clinton was set to pump more than £100m into Northern Ireland's economy to help turn political agreement into peace' (11 April 1998). A peaceful Northern Ireland would apparently enjoy the benefits of integration into the global free-market after years of Treasury subvention and economic stagnation. In the final phase of the referendum campaign, Nigel Smyth, director of the Confederation of British Industry (CBI) in Northern Ireland, affirmed the business community's support for the Agreement and mentioned a recent visit to Belfast by Virgin boss, Richard Branson, as part of the Yes campaign. For the CBI chief, Branson was a symbol of the entrepreneurship that peace and a political settlement could generate.[5] And in the wake of the referendum, with its overall majority Yes vote, a local newspaper headline signalled that it was the right result for business: 'Property pleased by yes' (*Irish News* 26 May 1998).

Film and television drama in this period also acknowledged the peace dividend. *An Everlasting Piece* (Levinson 2000) is set in the grim Belfast of the 1980s but posits cross-community entrepreneurship as the gateway to a new affluent environment. *With or Without You* (Winterbottom 1999) and *Wild About Harry* (Lowney 2000) set their stories of middle-class relationships against the backdrop of the new Belfast of 'urban renewal and brightly lit historic buildings. The iconography of both films is that of an affluent middle class with its culture of high-spend consumerism and metropolitan aspirations' (McLoone 2008: 59). Other dramas have been less enamoured by the promise of prosperity and enterprise. The television series, *Eureka Street* (BBC Northern Ireland 1999), is scathing of its vacuity and aware of its elisions. In a particularly pithy sequence, its unlikely hero, entrepreneur Chuckie Lurgan, closes a lucrative deal with an American businessman and announces it before a gathering of well-wishers and media on the steps of the beautifully illuminated Belfast City Hall. However, the camera rises to leave the celebrations and then arcs down onto the pavement, settling on a young newspaper seller who resembles Roche, the urchin boy Jake Jackson tries to help. On seeing the boy, Jake remarks that there are Roche look-alikes all over the city, an allusion perhaps to the widespread poverty and deprivation that still afflict large parts of the new Belfast. In the end, the lead characters in *Eureka Street* find redemption in romantic love, which apparently surpasses Northern Ireland's sectarian politics and the inanities of the new enterprise culture.

Eureka Street is not untypical of Northern Ireland on screen in this period, where ideological comfort is sought in domestic and personal relations. As we have seen in previous chapters, stories of 'housetrained' paramilitaries in fictions as diverse as *The Boxer* (Sheridan 1997), *The Mighty Celt* (Elliot 2005) and *Give My Head Peace* (BBC Northern Ireland 1996–2007) helped recuperate the image and reputation of former combatants and prepared the public for their entry into mainstream politics. On the other hand, as explored in chapter 5, associations with domesticity have had the effect of restricting the representation of 'ordinary people', mothers in particular, excluding them from engagement in politics and public activism. Yet, the disapprobation in which politics is held in Northern Ireland on screen sits comfortably with its entry into global capitalism. As Eric Hobsbawm has argued: 'Free-market theory effectively claims that there is no need for politics because the sovereignty of the consumer should prevail over everything else' (Hobsbawm 2000: 113). Seen in these terms, Northern Ireland is not only undergoing a peace process aimed at settling the conflict over its constitutional position, it is potentially undergoing a process of pacification, a denial of politics upon which the free market depends. This, then, is the implicit message of the propaganda of peace: advocating domesticated citizenship, consumer sovereignty and abstention from political activism while all the time assuring us that there is no alternative.

No alternatives?

Raymond Williams considered the 'structure of feeling' in any time and place as being 'a very deep and very wide possession [...] precisely because it is on it that communication depends' (Williams 1961: 65). However we do not mean to suggest that the emerging 'structure of feeling' associated with the peace process was so deep and wide that it was without its discontents or its alternative voices. The question is more whether these alternatives really mattered? Were they the best alternatives achievable at this critical moment in Northern Ireland's history?

We showed in chapter 2 that most loyalist and republican newspapers rejected the Good Friday Agreement outright, some of them unconvinced that peace was a self-evident good unless, of course, it could be achieved on their own exclusive terms. Yet their hostility extended beyond the immediate political settlement to the contemporary social and cultural milieu that they believed had facilitated the Agreement. Over the summer of 1998, the loyalist paper, *Warrior*, identified a range of foes determined to undermine the integrity of Ulster's union with Britain. They included former comrades and unionist politicians, the British and Irish governments, US President Bill Clinton, the Northern Ireland Office, the Labour Party, Marxists and socialists, the media and homosexuals. Its republican counterpart *Saoirse* had an equally impressive list of enemies. The front page of its June 1998 issue attacked the Yes campaign during the referendum, complaining that it had the advantage of a 'totally compliant' media. More than this, 'churches and schools were used as political platforms in some cases to urge acceptance of the Stormont Deal. Popstars and business millionaires were flown in to back up an internal settlement'. Arguably, the sometimes-cosmopolitan nature of these various enemies were also an affront to unreconstructed and narrowly defined ethno-nationalisms that *Saoirse* and *Warrior* articulated. Beleaguered and belligerent, they tended to view history as cyclical in its form, as no less than a long series of betrayals. This contrasts with the progressivist narrative preferred by the Ulster Museum in the *Up in Arms* exhibition and the local mainstream press at the time of the referendum.

Just as there is counter-propaganda there is also the potential to offer counter-hegemonic readings of the cultural material that has been presented in this book. Film and television drama in particular are more open to interpretation in this respect. For instance, it is possible to read a film like *Titanic Town* (Michell 1998) as an indictment of a society or culture that forces ordinary women like Bernie McPhelimy to chose between her family and public life. Indeed, on one level, the film has the potential to say something rather intriguing about the ambiguous and onerous responsibilities of women and mothers. Bernie's initial involvement in the peace campaign is clearly motivated by a sense of maternal responsibility for the protection of her children; as she says in a radio interview, her right to speak out and campaign on the issue of violence derives from her 'authority as a mother'. However, the film subverts her authority through the eyes of her daughter, Annie, who sees things rather differently. She berates her mother's commitment to the peace movement when it appears to make the family more rather than less vulnerable to attack. When Bernie retorts, 'How dare you make me responsible!' Annie has the last word: 'You *are* responsible, y'cow'. In this respect the film explores the inherent contradiction between Bernie's sense of responsibility as a mother entrusted with her children's safety and well-being, and her liability for the violence that is visited upon the family during the peace campaign. 'Oh, for Christ's sake!' she exclaims at one point in the film. 'Why is everyone making me responsible for everything that happens?' Her abdication of domestic obligations is striking as it is so uncharacteristic but her objection to her treatment does not stop there. In her final public appearance, standing on the steps of Stormont before the media, Bernie meets every question with a simple 'no comment'. Her relative silence at this point seems like a form of protest against the political sophistry that has corrupted her good intentions.[6]

It is possible, then, to read *Titanic Town*, as a subversive commentary on the contradictions that confront Bernie as a mother and an activist but also as an indictment of a political culture that can find no place for a woman. However, two critical aspects of the film militate against such a counter-hegemonic reading. Firstly, its depiction of a hostile, sometimes violent political sphere leaves Bernie with nowhere else to go but home; and secondly, given the sheer weight of preference for domesticated citizenship in recent films about Northern Ireland generally, it would be perverse to read the film in any other terms than its denial and disparagement of politics.

The notion in many of the films and television dramas we have looked at that we can simply 'close the front door on the chaos out there', is a predominantly middle-class privilege. Dan Starkey does this in *Divorcing Jack* (Caffrey 1998) once he is re-united with his wife. Likewise in *With or Without You*, married, middle-class Protestants, Vincent and Rosie, seem alienated by choice from the new dispensation. Vincent has left the police at Rosie's bidding and now works for his father-in-law. Missing the excitement and comradeship of his old job, he cuts a rather emasculated figure, an impression heightened by the question mark over his fertility. Rosie is utterly disaffected with her job as receptionist in the new Waterfront Hall and is desperate to conceive. Belfast is rendered as a cosmopolitan tourist attraction but its potential and its pleasures seem to be undermined by the couple's sterility, both literal and metaphorical. Their attempts to resuscitate old relationships bring them no satisfaction but the news that Rosie is at last pregnant reconciles them to each other and their environment. This is illustrated by the final scene at the baby's christening when the couple are photographed at the centre of their previously cantankerous extended family and friends.

No such reconciliation is possible in *As the Beast Sleeps* (Bradbeer 2002). Loyalist paramilitaries, Freddie and Kyle, rail against the new realities of the peace process and the ceasefire, specifically the new enterprising brand of political loyalism that usurps them. While both *With or Without You* and *As the Beast Sleeps* offer representations of characters discomforted in the new environment, the conventions of romantic comedy in *Without or Without You* allow its middle-class protagonists to transcend it, reconcile themselves to it, or find compensation in intimacy. The social-realist conventions that drive *As the Beast Sleeps*, on the other hand, offer no such 'happy ending' for its characters. In fact, the new political realities that constrain and even overwhelm them in the political sphere also tear asunder their fragile private relationships and domestic arrangements. For Kyle and Freddie, the peace process offers no alternative and no hope.

Of all the film and television dramas we have considered in this volume, *As the Beast Sleeps* is a rare exception in that it allows no easy separation of political and private life. The conceit that one can has deprived film and television drama of the ability to deal in any real sense with political issues at a critical time in Northern Ireland's history. It certainly marks a significant ideological shift in cinematic representation from the period just before the ceasefires and peace process. For instance, Joe Comerford's *Reefer and the Model* (1987) and *High Boot Benny* (1993), and Thaddeus O'Sullivan's *December Bride* (1991) radically re-imagined personal relationships and challenged conservative notions of community and nationhood. The renegades and misfits in Comerford's films are provocative alternatives to traditional versions of Irish nationalism, while Thaddeus O'Sullivan's *ménage à trois* in *December Bride* offer an affront to patriarchy and religious, communal conformity. Martin McLoone argues that this work was typical of 'a cinema of national questioning' (McLoone 1994: 168).

Conclusion

We might have assumed that the censorious and reactionary cultural atmosphere before the peace process would have made it more difficult to say something critical or subversive in the media about society in Northern Ireland. Ironically, it is the new dispensation that has quashed politically engaged film and television drama and impoverished the cultural imagination. Far from prompting serious public debate about what kind of society could or should emerge out of a constitutional settlement of the conflict, the peace process has instead been marked by the simple imperative of pacification. The construction of a peace process 'consensus' has somehow pre-empted the need or desire to question, re-imagine or propose alternatives at a critical moment in history.

As Eric Hobsbawm points out when considering the prospects for war and peace in the twenty-first century, 'the more rapidly growing inequalities created by uncontrolled free-market globalisation are natural incubators of grievance and instability' (Hobsbawm 2008: 42). He was writing at a time when the neo-liberal project seemed unassailable but the credit crunch and the financial meltdown of September 2008 have thrown it into a crisis of legitimacy that, as Antonio Gramsci explained, gives rise to 'a great variety of morbid symptoms' (Gramsci 1971: 276). In the specific context of Northern Ireland, such symptoms include increasing sectarian conflict, social exclusion and poverty. As journalist David McKittrick has reported, a total of 1500 sectarian attacks – an average of four a day – took place in the space of one year, 2008/09. Meanwhile, the number of families evacuated from their homes because of intimidation had also risen in that period.[7] For many people living in low-income, interface areas, the domestic sphere offers little or no respite from sectarian violence. Yet these realities have barely been acknowledged in the media and cultural representations we have considered in this volume. Instead, the overwhelming emphasis of the propaganda of peace has been a discourse of 'no alternative' – effectively a denial of politics in preference for domesticated consumerism – just at a time when what is really needed in Northern Ireland, post devolution, is politically engaged public discourse and active citizenship.

Notes

1. Clinton, W. J. (1998), 'The Northern Ireland Peace Accord Referendum', *Clinton Radio Remarks*, http://ftp.resource.org/gpo.gov/papers/1998/1998_vol1_834.pdf. Accessed 20 August 2009.
2. Boyd, S., 11 August 2004 interview.
3. BBC Northern Ireland (1998), *Hearts and Minds*, 15 October.
4. BBC Northern Ireland (1998), *Hearts and Minds*, 29 October.
5. Anon. (1998), 'CBI chief points to yes boost: Deal "paves way to prosperity"', *Belfast Telegraph*, 21 May.
6. Silence as a form of female protest has an antecedent in Irish cinema. *Anne Devlin* (Murphy 1984), the story of a servant in the house of Irish rebel leader, Robert Emmet, recalls its eponymous heroine's retreat into silence as means of avoiding informing on Emmet to her British captors.
7. 'The enduring scar of sectarianism', *The Independent*, 14 September 2009.

Bibliography

Appleton. D. (1999), *The Most Fertile Man in Ireland*.

Baker, K. (1996), 'Reporting the Conflict', in M. McLoone (ed.), *Broadcasting in a Divided Community: Seventy Years of the BBC in Northern Ireland*, Belfast: Institute of Irish Studies, pp. 118–126.

Baker, S. (2001), 'Imagining Ulster in the Modern World', Ph.D. thesis, Coleraine: University Of Ulster at Coleraine.

Baker, S. (2004), 'Vampire Troubles: Loyalism and Resurrection Man', in R. Barton and H. O'Brien (eds.), *Keeping it Real: Irish Film and Television*, London: Wallflower Press, pp. 78–86.

Barton, R. (2004), *Irish National Cinema*, London: Routledge.

Barton, R. and O'Brien, H. (eds.) (2004), *Keeping it Real: Irish Film and Television*, London: Wallflower Press.

BBC (1985), 'At the Edge of the Union', *Real Lives*.

BBC (1997), *Provos*.

BBC (1999), *Loyalists*.

BBC (2000), *Brits*.

BBC (2006), *Facing the Truth*.

BBC Northern Ireland (1982), *Too Late to Talk to Billy*.

BBC Northern Ireland (1983), *A Matter of Choice for Billy*.

BBC Northern Ireland (1984), *A Coming to Terms for Billy*.

BBC Northern Ireland (1986–1987), *Foreign Bodies*.

BBC Northern Ireland (1989-1991), *The Show*.

BBC Northern Ireland (1991), *So You Think You've Got Troubles*.

BBC Northern Ireland (1994), *The Empire Laughs Back*.

BBC Northern Ireland (1995), *Two Ceasefires and a Wedding*.

BBC Northern Ireland (1996–2007), *Give My Head Peace*.

BBC Northern Ireland (1999), *Eureka Street*.

BBC Northern Ireland (2002), *Somme Journey*.

Bell, D. (1998), 'Modernising history: The real politik of heritage and cultural tradition in Northern Ireland', in D. Miller (ed.), *Rethinking Northern Ireland: Culture, Ideology and Colonialism*, London: Longman.

Bennett, T. (1995), *The Birth of the Museum: History, Theory, Politics*, London: Routledge.

Ben-Porat, G. (2005), 'Between power and hegemony; business communities in peace processes', *Review of International Studies*, 31, pp. 325–348.

Bolton, R. (1996), 'Death on the Rock', in B. Rolston and D. Miller (eds.), *War and Words: the Northern Ireland Media Reader*, Belfast: Beyond the Pale, pp. 118–141.

Bradbeer, H. (2002), *As the Beast Sleeps*.

Brett, D. (1996), *The Construction of Heritage*, Cork: Cork University Press.

Brozel, M. (2003), *Holy Cross*.

Butler, D. (1995), *The Trouble with Reporting Northern Ireland*, Aldershot: Avebury Publishing.

Caffrey, D. (1998), *Divorcing Jack*.

Cairns, E., Wilson R., Gallagher T. and Trew, K. (1995), 'Psychology's Contribution to Understanding Conflict in Northern Ireland', *Peace and Conflict: Journal of Peace Psychology*, 1: 2, pp. 131–148.

Cathcart, R. (1984), *The Most Contrary Region: the BBC in Northern Ireland, 1924-1984*, Belfast: Blackstaff Press.

Comerford, J. (1987), *Reefer and the Model*.

Comerford, J. (1994), *High Boot Benny*.

Crooke, E. (2001), 'Confronting a Troubled History: which past in Northern Ireland's museums?', *International Journal of Heritage Studies*, 7:2, pp. 119–136.

Curtis, L. (1988), *Ireland, The Propaganda War: The British Media and the 'Battle for Hearts and Minds'*, Belfast: Sasta.

Curtis, L. (1996), 'A catalogue of censorship, 1959–1993', in W. Rolston and D. Miller (eds.), *War and Words: the Northern Ireland Media Reader*, Belfast: Beyond the Pale, pp. 265–304.

Elliott, P. (2005), *The Mighty Celt*.

Evans, M. (1998), *Resurrection Man*.

Foster, R. F. (2001), *The Irish Story: Telling Tales and Making It Up in Ireland*, London: Allen Lane.

Francis, R. (1996), 'Broadcasting to a Community in Conflict – The Experience of Northern Ireland', in B. Rolston and D. Miller (eds.), *War and Words: the Northern Ireland Media Reader*, Belfast: Beyond the Pale, pp. 56–66.

George, T. (1996), *Some Mother's Son*.

Gramsci, A. (1971), *Selections from the Prison Notebooks*, London: Lawrence and Wishart.

Gray, J. (1988), *The Sans Culottes of Belfast: The United Irishmen and the Men of No Property*, Belfast: Belfast Trades Union Council/The United Irishmen Commemorative Society.

Harvey, D. (2008), 'The Right to the City', *New Left Review*, 53, September–October, pp. 23–40.

Henderson, L., Reilly J. and Miller, D. (1990), 'Speak No Evil: The British Broadcasting Ban, The Media, and the Conflict in Ireland', Research Report, Glasgow: Glasgow University Media Group.

Hennessey, T. (2000), *The Northern Ireland Peace Process: Ending the Troubles?*, Dublin: Gill and Macmillan.

Hill, J. (1987), 'Images of Violence', in K. Rockett, L. Gibbons and J. Hill (eds.), *Cinema and Ireland*, London: Croom Helm, pp. 147–193.

Hill, J. (2006), *Cinema and Northern Ireland: Film, Culture and Politics*, London: BFI.

Hill, J., McLoone, M. and Hainsworth, P. (eds.) (1994), *Border Crossing: Film in Ireland, Britain and Europe*, Belfast: Institute of Irish Studies/British Film Institute.

Hirschbiegel, O. (2009), *Five Minutes of Heaven*.

Hobsbawm, E. (1975), *The Age of Capital 1848-1875*, London: Weidenfeld and Nicolson.

Hobsbawm, E. (2000), *The New Century*, London: Little, Brown.

Hobsbawm, E. (2008), *Globalisation, Democracy and Terrorism*, London: Abucus.

Jack, I. (1988), 'Gibraltar', *Granta*, 25, Autumn, pp. 14–86.

Jackson, A. (1995), 'Irish Unionist Imagery', in E. Patton (ed.), *Returning to Ourselves*, Belfast: Lagan Press.

Jordan, N. (1997), *The Butcher Boy*.

Kyle, K. (1996), 'The Media and Northern Ireland: Some Personal Reflections 1969–80', in M. McLoone (ed.), *Broadcasting in a Divided Community: Seventy Years of the BBC in Northern Ireland*. Belfast: Institute of Irish Studies, pp. 105–117.

Leapman, M. (1996), 'The "Real Lives" Controversy', in B. Rolston and D. Miller (eds.), *War and Words: the Northern Ireland Media Reader*, Belfast: Beyond the Pale, pp. 96–117.

Levinson, B. (2000), *An Everlasting Piece*.

Loane, T. (2004), *Mickybo and Me*.

Lowney, D. (2000), *Wild About Harry*.

MacDonald, S. J. (2003), 'Museums, national, postnational and transcultural identities', *Museum and Society*, 1:1, pp. 1–16.

MacGinty, R. and Darby, J. (2002), *Guns and Government: The Management of the Northern Ireland Peace Process*, Basingstoke: Palgrave Macmillan.

Mallie, E. and McKittrick, D. (1996), *The Fight for Peace: The Secret Story Behind the Irish Peace Process*, London: Heinemann.

Marx, K. [1852] (2000), 'The Eighteenth Brumaire of Louis Napoleon', in D. McLellan (ed.), *Karl Marx: Selected Writings*, Oxford: Oxford University Press.

McDowell, R. G. (1998), 'Sell-out or compromise', *Orange Standard*, May.

McIlroy, B. (1998), *Shooting to Kill: Filmmaking and the 'Troubles' in Northern Ireland*, Trowbridge: Flicks Books.

McKittrick, D. (1996), *The Nervous Peace*, Belfast: Blackstaff Press.

McLaughlin, G. (2000), 'Television current affairs: the case of Northern Ireland', in J. Weiten, G. Murdock and P. Dahlgren (eds.), *Television Across Europe: A Comparative Introduction*, London: Sage, pp. 220–235.

McLaughlin, G. (2006), 'Profits, Politics and Paramilitaries: The local news media in Northern Ireland', in Bob Franklin (ed.), *Local Journalism and Local Media: Making the Local News*, London: Routledge, pp. 60–69.

McLaughlin, G. (2009), 'Changing Hearts and Minds? Television, paramilitaries and the peace process', in J. J. Popiolkowski and N. Cull (eds.), *Public Diplomacy, Cultural Interventions in the Peace Process in Northern Ireland*, Los Angeles: Figueroa Press, pp. 43–55.

McLaughlin, G. and Miller, D. (1996), 'The Media Politics of the Irish Peace Process', *International Journal Press/Politics*, 1: 4, pp. 116–134.

McLoone, M. (1993), 'The Commitments: the NIO anti-terrorist ads', *Fortnight*, 321, October, pp. 34–36.

McLoone, M. (1994), 'National Cinema and Cultural Identity: Ireland and Europe', in J. Hill, M. McLoone and P. Hainsworth (eds.), *Border Crossings: Film in Ireland, Britain and Europe*, Belfast: Institute of Irish Studies/British Film Institute, pp. 146–173.

McLoone, M. (1996), 'Drama out of a Crisis: BBC Television Drama and the Northern Ireland Troubles', in M. McLoone (ed.), *Broadcasting in a Divided Community: Seventy Years of the BBC in Northern Ireland*, Belfast: Institute of Irish Studies, pp. 73–104.

McLoone, M. (1997), 'What kind of peace', in *Willie Doherty, Same Old Story*, Colchester: firstsite, pp. 23–26.

McLoone, M. (2000), *Irish Film: The Emergence of a Contemporary Cinema*, London: British Film Institute, p. 78.

McLoone, M. (2008), *Film, Media and Popular Culture in Ireland: Cityscapes, Landscapes, Soundscapes*, Dublin: Irish Academic Press.

Michell, R. (1998), *Titanic Town*.

Miller, D. (1993), 'Official Sources and "primary definition": the case of Northern Ireland', *Media, Culture and Society*, 15:3, London: Sage, pp. 385–405.

Miller, D. (1994), *Don't Mention the War: Northern Ireland, Propaganda and the Media*, London: Pluto.

Miller, D. (ed.) (1998), *Rethinking Northern Ireland: culture, ideology and colonialism*, London: Longman.

Miller, D. (2002), 'The media, propaganda, and the Northern Ireland peace process', in D. Kiberd (ed.), *Media in Ireland: Issues in broadcasting*, Dublin: Four Courts Press, pp. 114–129.

Mitchell, G. (1999), *Making Peace: The inside story of the making of the Good Friday Agreement*, London: Heinemann.

Moore, P. (2003), 'Legacy. Fourth Phase public service broadcasting in Northern Ireland', *The Radio Journal*, 1: 2, pp. 87–100.

Muldoon, O. T. (2004), 'Children of the Troubles: The Impact of Political Violence in Northern Ireland', *Journal of Social Issues*, 60: 3, pp. 453–468.

Murphy, P. (1984), *Anne Devlin*.

Nairn, T. (1977), The *Break-Up of Britain: Crisis and Neo-Nationalism*, London: Verso.

Neale, S. and Krutnik, F. (1990), *Popular Film and Television Comedy*, London: Routledge.

Nesbitt, N. (1979), *A Museum in Belfast: a history of the Ulster Museum and its predecessors*, Belfast: Ulster Museum.

Northern Ireland Office (1988), *A Future*.

Northern Ireland Office (1993), *Lady*.

Northern Ireland Office (1993), *I Wanna Be Like You*.

Northern Ireland Office (1994), *A New Era*.

Northern Ireland Office (1995), *Northern Irish Difference*.

Northern Ireland Office (1995), *Northern Irish Life*.

Northern Ireland Office (1995), *Northern Irish Quality*.

Northern Ireland Office (1995), *Northern Irish Spirit*.

O'Carroll, L. (2005), 'The truth behind Real Lives', *Media Guardian*, 12 December, p. 3.

O'Clery, C. (1996), *The Greening of the White House: the inside story of how America tried to bring peace to Ireland*, Dublin: Gill and Macmillan.

O'Rawe, M. (2008), 'Policing change: to reform or not to transform?', in C. Coulter and M. Murray (eds.), *Northern Ireland After the Troubles. A Society in Transition*, Manchester: Manchester University Press, pp. 110–132.

O'Sullivan, T. (1991), *December Bride*.

O'Sullivan, T. (1996), *Nothing Personal*.

Parkinson, A. F. (1998), *Ulster Loyalism and the British Media*, Dublin: Four Courts Press.

Pettitt, L. (2000), *Screening Ireland: Film and Television Representation*, Manchester: Manchester University Press.

Purdy, M. (2005), *Room 21: Stormont – Behind Closed Doors*, Belfast: Brehon Press.

Reed, C. (1947), *Odd Man Out*.

Rockett, K., Gibbons L. and Hill J. (1987), *Cinema and Ireland*, London: Croom Helm.

Rolston, B. (ed.) (1991), *The Media and Northern Ireland: Covering the Troubles*, Basingstoke: Palgrave Macmillan.

Rolston, B. (1992), *Drawing Support: Murals in the North of Ireland*, Belfast: Beyond the Pale.

Rolston, B. (1995), *Drawing Support 2: Murals of War and Peace*, Belfast: Beyond the Pale.

Rolston, B. (2003), *Drawing Support 3: Murals and Transition in the North of Ireland*, Belfast: Beyond the Pale.

Rolston, B. (2007), 'Facing Reality: The media, the past and conflict transformation in Northern Ireland', *Crime, Media, Culture*, 3:3, London: Sage, pp. 345–364.

Rolston, B. and D. Miller (eds.) (1996), *War and Words: the Northern Ireland Media Reader*, Belfast: Beyond the Pale.

Rowthorn, B. (1987), 'Northern Ireland: an economy in crisis', in P. Teague (ed.), *Beyond the rhetoric: politics, economy and social policy in Northern Ireland*, London: Lawrence and Wishart, pp. 111–135.

RTÉ (1994), *The Late, Late Show*.

Schlesinger, P., Murdock, G. and Elliott, P. (1983), *Televising 'Terrorism': political violence in popular culture*, London: Sage.

Sennett, R. (1977), *The Fall of Public Man*, London: Penguin.

Sheridan, J. (1997), *The Boxer*.

Spencer, G. (2000), *Disturbing the Peace? Politics, Television News and the Northern Ireland Peace Process*, London: Ashgate.

Spencer, G. (2001), 'Keeping the peace? Politics, television news and the Northern Ireland peace process', *Irish Journal of Sociology*, 10: 2, pp. 57–76.

Thames Television (1988), 'Death on the Rock', *This Week*.

Travis, P. (2004), *Omagh*.

Ulster Museum (1990), *Kings in Conflict: Ireland in the 1690s catalogue*, Belfast: Ulster Museum.

Ulster Museum (1998), *Up in Arms: The 1798 Rebellion in Ireland catalogue*, Belfast: Ulster Museum.

Ulster Museum (1998), *Up in Arms: The 1798 Rebellion in Ireland exhibition guide*, Belfast: Ulster Museum.

Ulster Museum (2004), *Conflict: The Irish at War exhibition guide*, Belfast: Ulster Museum.

Vergo, P. (ed.) (1989), *The New Museology*, London: Reaktion Books.

Williams, R. (1961), *The Long Revolution*, London: The Hogarth Press.

Williams, R. (1966), *Modern Tragedy*, London: Chatto and Windus.

Williams, R. (1977), *Marxism and Literature*, Oxford: Oxford University Press.

Williams, R. (1979), *Politics and Letters: Interviews with New Left Review*, London: New Left Books.

Winterbottom, M. (1993), *Love Lies Bleeding*.

Winterbottom, M. (1999), *With or Without You*.

Wolfsfeld, G. (2004), *Media and the Path to Peace*, London: Cambridge University Press.

Zavarzadeh, M. (1991), *Seeing Films Politically*, New York: State University of New York Press.

Index